4-WEEK LOAN

SANTA MONICA
PUBLIC
LIBRARY

www.smpl.org

TELEPHONE RENEWALS:
Main Library. 451-1866
Ocean Park Branch 392-3804
Fairview Branch 450-0443
Montana Branch 829-7081

DATE DUE

ZAPATA'S DISCIPLE

Essays

ZAPATA'S DISCIPLE

Essays

by Martín Espada

South End Press
Cambridge, MA

Cover photo: Frank Espada, "'Reagan le roba a los pobres'"
    (Washington, D.C., 1981)
Cover design by Beth Fortune
Printed in the U.S.A.

Library of Congress Cataloging-in-Publication Data
Espada, Martín, 1957-
Zapata's disciple : essays / by Martín Espada.
      p. cm.
ISBN 0-89608-590-2 (cloth). — ISBN 0-89608-589-9 (pbk.)
I. Title.
PS3555.S53Z36 1998
814'.54—dc21   98-17384
                                                          CIP

South End Press, 7 Brookline Street, #1, Cambridge, MA 02139
04 03 02 01 00 99 98   1 2 3 4 5 6 7

This book is dedicated to my father

Contents

I. ZAPATA'S DISCIPLE

Zapata's Disciple
and Perfect Brie

In December 1949, in Biloxi, Mississippi, my father was arrested for not going to the back of the bus. A darkskinned Puerto Rican raised in New York, he did not accept the laws of Jim Crow. A judge sentenced him to a week in jail. This is what he learned: 1) he would be branded for the rest of his life by the brown pigment of his skin; and 2) he would fight. He would rather sit in jail than at the back of the bus.

My father's social class was defined by the opportunities denied him because of racism, and the opportunities he created for himself in spite of racism; the assignment of a servile status based on skin color, and his furious rejection of that status, for himself and others. His experiences—the frustrations and rages, the stubborn resistance, the dignity of his defiance—formed the environment in which I evolved, as son and poet, contributing to my awareness of class and its punishments.

3

What most damaged my father was the lack of a college education. Instead, there was a succession of jobs and places. Mechanic in the Air Force, a training he was not permitted to use as a civilian in the segregated airline industry. A grocery store, which he abandoned after pulling a gun on thugs demanding protection money. Semiprofessional baseball. A sanitation crew cleaning the Holland Tunnel in New York, where he fell off a truck and injured his back. There may have been music somewhere: A family legend tells of drums sold to pay the rent. Or writing: A typewriter, hocked many times, didn't come back one day. When I was born, in 1957, he was working for an electrical contractor, and by all accounts hating it.

Political activism was his salvation. He began by organizing in his own community, the East New York section of Brooklyn. He organized rent strikes, voter registration drives, sit-ins of welfare mothers, marches for safe streets and civil rights. He was a fierce stump speaker, who once shared a podium at a rally with Malcolm X. He went to jail again. He was that most dangerous of creatures, a working-class radical. James Graham, in *The Enemies of the Poor*, compared my father to a guerrilla-disciple of Emiliano Zapata, the Mexican revolutionary.

He rose through the political ranks in New York City, directing a series of community-based organizations and programs. At the height of his influence as a leader, he walked away from the wars. He had always been a photographer, and in the late 1970s a grant enabled him to create the Puerto Rican Diaspora Documentary Project, a photo-documentary and oral history of the Puerto Rican migration across the United States. He is still a photographer today.

I spent my childhood in working-class housing projects in East New York. The projects were not yet the stereotypical swamps breeding the malaria of crime and drugs, but projects nevertheless, dreary institutional housing, the urban reservation meant to confine the urban savage. The environment was full of paranoia and tinged with violence: A grocer murdered in a robbery, a friend beaten and stripped by a local gang. Yet, in this environment, I was raised with an ethos of resistance all around me. Some of my earliest drawings depict demonstrations, sketched on the back of flyers announcing those same demonstrations. I remember, from the age of eight, a march and candlelight vigil for a short-order cook kicked to death by junkies, a spontaneous outpouring of grief and compassion burned so deeply into my imagination that I wrote a poem about it over twenty years later: "The Moon Shatters on Alabama Avenue."

As my father moved from blue-collar to white-collar work, our social status changed. We left the projects. However, being Puerto Rican in effect canceled out whatever middle-class trappings we had acquired for ourselves. In a Long Island high school, surrounded by the children of white flight, I faced racial obscenities everywhere, spray-painted on my locker and even scrawled in the icing on a cake. The brawls were inevitable: Being kicked repeatedly in a classroom while the teacher looked away, or having my head slammed into a water fountain. Here, the gangs were called fraternities.

Not coincidentally, at this time I began to write poetry, as an attempt to explain myself to myself. This writing, however, was not for the consumption of teachers, or for school. I was a spectacularly marginal student. In fact, I was so seriously alienated that I once failed English. I failed

Typing, too, but that was because I was tapping out poems instead of the Quick Brown Fox, etc.

In the recession of the 1970s and early 1980s, I wandered in and out of school, from job to job. This is my résumé: janitor at Sears, bindery worker in a printing plant, gas station attendant, door-to-door encyclopedia salesman, pizza cook, telephone solicitor, car washer for a factory showroom, bouncer in a bar, caretaker in a primate laboratory, night desk clerk in a transient hotel, worker on a cleaning crew for a minor league ballpark, radio journalist in Nicaragua, patient rights advocate in Wisconsin mental hospitals, and welfare rights paralegal, among other jobs. I was not in the business of collecting colorful anecdotes; when I took a job, I was always in need of a job. Recently, an interviewer asked why I chose to work as a bouncer. Because I thought it would look good when I came up for tenure, I said.

Working was better than not working. I sampled a wide variety of social service programs. I unraveled food vouchers like Roman scrolls in checkout lines. I marveled at the irony of Jefferson signing the Declaration of Independence on my food stamps. I sold the ring on my finger. I stood in line for General Relief, and found myself next to a former client, recently released from a mental hospital. Who are you here for, he wanted to know. Me, I said. To borrow a phrase from Herbert Hill, I have been both a client and a constituent.

Like my father, I refused to accept my place in line. I obtained a law degree from Northeastern University Law School, and worked as an attorney for a number of years. I, too, channeled my energy into political activism. I practiced bilingual education law with META (Multicultural Education, Training and Advocacy, Inc.), and served as Supervisor of Su Clínica Legal, a legal services program for low-income, Spanish-speaking tenants in Chelsea, outside Boston. Now I work as a Professor in the English Department at the University of Massachusetts–Amherst, teaching creative writing and Latino poetry. Given my history, I ask myself: What next? Chimney sweep? Rodeo clown?

~~~

For some poets, social class is the triangle in the orchestra, a distant tinkling. For me, the matter of social class is the beat itself, an insistent percussion (mine is a Latin jazz orchestra). In writing about social class, I pay homage, bear witness, act as advocate, and tell secrets.

I pay homage, for example, when I write about my father's struggles. My poem "The Other Alamo" deals with his sit-in at a segregated lunch counter in San Antonio, Texas, for the privilege of being served a cheeseburger. I want to confront the complacency of those who take their privileges for granted with the news of this event. I also want to comfort those who have endured similar humiliations, hold a mirror to their faces, show them the pride there.

Paying homage is about the acceptance of an inheritance, the refusal to forsake ancestors, community, class.

I bear witness when I write about my work experiences. For many years, I was a spy. Since laborers are invisible in many eyes, valued only for what their hands can do, people say and do things in front of them which reveal true motivations, unspoken bigotries. My boss at the factory showroom felt free to ask me why the spics at his Air Force base always cut the lunch line, because I wasn't really there for him. This invisibility has been a blessing for me. As a poet-spy, I not only saw and heard, but saw and heard differently from the people around me. As I pumped gas, no one was aware that I would write a poem about the intoxicated hearse driver who asked me directions. As I hosed down cages coated with monkeyshit, no one could predict that I would write a poem called "Do Not Put Dead Monkeys in the Freezer." The drunk I punched in the head as a bar bouncer, breaking my finger, certainly didn't anticipate I would write a poem about him. Neither did the judge in Chelsea District Court, where I argued as a lawyer, realize that I would someday write verse comparing his face to a fist.

I am an advocate when I write poems speaking on behalf of those without an opportunity to be heard, for one of the curses of segregation and subordination by class is the imposition of silence. The poems seek to release a voice caught in the collective throat. Here, I am influenced by a long Latin American tradition: Pablo Neruda, Ernesto Cardenal, Clemente Soto Vélez, Claribel Alegría. Eduardo Galeano has written, "I write for those who cannot read me." These are the human beings who, in the words of Wolfgang Binder, "run the risk of leaving this earth unrecorded." If I know Mrs. Báez, a Dominican immigrant living in the burned-out wreckage of a building torched by her landlord, then I am obligated to record her painfully dignified ritual of serving coffee to strangers. If I know Jacobo Mena, a Guatemalan artist, a refugee from political persecution on the verge of being deported, who cleaned offices by night and painted stunning landscapes by day, I am compelled to write of his colors, his green and red. To know that a cockroach may become embedded in a child's ear is to accept responsibility for that knowledge, to communicate that knowledge for the sake of those who do not know, and those who do. How could I know what I know, and not tell what I know?

I tell secrets when I write about social class. The great secret is that class matters, very much, in this society dizzy with the illusion of classlessness. Writing about class is to write about power relationships as they really are, in their nakedness, and so to write about how this system actually works. And where better to learn about the emphasis on property over people than in court, with landlord-tenant cases? The poem, "Tires Stacked in the Hallways of Civilization," documents an actual exchange in Chelsea District Court, where a landlord admitted that there were rodents infesting the building, but justified himself by proclaiming that he allowed the tenant to have a cat. I call this my cat poem.

In the words of critic Thomas Disch, "Class distinctions are the great dividing line in American poetry, all the more divisive for being, officially, invisible." Far too many poets maintain the myth of a society without any real class distinctions or conflict. They do so by assuming that everyone belongs to a certain elite, and writing accordingly, with an elitist diction full of elitist references for elite audiences, revealing their class biases in unintended, and, for me, unflattering ways. Once, while judging a national poetry competition, I came across a series of vacation poems (as distinct from travel poems), written by a poet who bragged that she went to Paris and "lunched on perfect Brie." The arrogance and snobbery of that statement simply dazzled me. I was reminded of lines from Neruda, speaking of a fellow poet who ate bread every day, but had never seen a baker.

Not everyone belongs to the elite, even in the world of poetry. The damned are not only subject, but also audience, and even poets themselves. Not every poetry reading occurs on a college campus, at a bookstore or cafe. There are readings and workshops at community centers and prisons, for adult literacy/GED and ESL (English as a Second Language) programs, at nursing homes and reservations. Not every poet works, or has always worked, as an academic.

Some poets are poets of the kitchen. Their lives are fogged with sweat, loud with the noise of their labor. To be heard over the crashing of pots, these poets may shout, in a language understood by the other workers in the kitchen, to remind them of their humanity even in the midst of flames. As always with kitchen work, many of the poets are dark-skinned or female; there may be no English, or a new English. The kitchen, for these poets, may literally be a city jail, a welfare office, a housing project, a factory, or a migrant labor camp. Even those not born of the kitchen, but somehow caught in its chaos, breathe the same heat, learn the same songs, and then testify. What they all have to say and how they say it reflect the turbulence of this existence, past and present. Their poetry has the capacity to create solidarity among those in the kitchen and empathy among those outside the kitchen.

There are so many poets, in the Latino community alone, who write from the kitchen with grace and power. Jack Agüeros of East Harlem gives us *Sonnets from the Puerto Rican,* demanding respect for his street subjects with the use of the sonnet form. Luis Rodríguez writes of "La Vida Loca," his gang days in Chicano East Los Angeles. Enid Santiago Welch records the ritual interrogations of welfare, and Lorna Dee Cervantes recalls growing up in "a woman-family" where she translated the same welfare notices. Frank Lima and Jimmy Santiago Baca sing of their resilient humanity as survivors of the prison experience. Gary Soto, Tino Villanueva, and Diana García evoke childhood in a migrant farmworker family. Demetria Martínez has documented the realities of two Salvadoran refugee women in her poem, "Nativity," and was prosecuted for allegedly smuggling "aliens" (she was acquitted, despite the fact that the poem was introduced against her as evidence).

Then there are the poets no one has read: Jesús Rangel, a boy from Michoacán, México, I encountered in an Oregon high school workshop, who wrote of his farmworker experience, "There is no gold / But feathers / At Lynden Farms"; another boy, introduced to me as "Brandon" at a reading in a Boston juvenile detention center, who was so dedicated to his poetry that he would provoke brawls with the other inmates and be thrown into solitary confinement, where he could write in relative tranquility.

All of us write about class, not as abstraction, not with a capital C, but as a consequence of lived experience. As with any other poet, our poems are about family, friends, lovers, clients, community, self. The difference is that the people in these poems suffer from the class system rather than benefit by it.

All this is not to say that a poet who writes about these issues must necessarily forgo the concerns of language. There is no contradiction between writing about being poor, or working-class, or Latino, and writing well. When we write about the collisions of class, we are writing about conflict, and we were always told in school that conflict was at the heart of good literature. Perhaps the vocabulary is more urgent than usual, but then again the house is on fire.

What do we want, finally, when we write from an awareness of class and its punishments? We want change, which, as Frederick Douglass pointed out, does not come without a demand. This is the poem as an act of political imagination, the poet not merely as prosecutor, but as visionary. For this purpose, a poem can be as useful as a hammer. I think of all the reversals I want to see, the reversals of a poem called "Imagine the Angels of Bread": squatters evicting landlords, refugees deporting judges, immigrants crossing the border to be greeted with trumpets and drums, the food stamps of adolescent mothers auctioned like gold doubloons. I think of my father, and the peace that has never been his. Here is my vision: the war is over, and Zapata's disciple is lunching on perfect Brie.

Postcard from
the Empire of Queen Ixolib

~ ~

Recently, I made a pilgrimage to a parking lot at the corner of Main Street and Howard Avenue in Biloxi, Mississippi, across from the Masonic Temple.

Almost fifty years ago, a few days before Christmas, a Trailways bus stopped at around midnight in this town on the Gulf of México. A young man, nineteen years old, born in Puerto Rico, slept in the seat immediately behind the driver, the only passenger on the bus, en route to visit his family in New York City. He was wearing a Class A khaki uniform from the Air Force, having finished four months of basic training at Lackland Air Force base in San Antonio. His dark skin was darker still after his time in the omnipotent Texas heat. He must have been tired, which may explain why he did not stir in Biloxi until he was shaken awake.

A new bus driver was poking him. The driver said: "You have to get to the back of the bus." The airman muttered, "Fuck you," and waved the driver away, then tilted his cap over his eyes. A few minutes later, he awoke to a flashlight bleaching his face, exploring the geography of his skin. A huge police officer said: "It's time for you to go." He was arrested and taken in a police car to the local jail; it was the first time he had ever been arrested. He was not fingerprinted, photographed, or allowed a phone call. He noticed that everyone in jail was Black.

The following day, the airman stood before a justice of the peace. He had no lawyer. The judge was white-haired, with the jowls of a bloodhound, oozing eyes that stared down over bifocals, and a dangling string tie. The judge lectured on respect for the law and the local custom of segregation, then asked: "Boy, how many days you have on that furlough?" This was a ten-day furlough, before the next assignment at an Air Force base in Illinois. The judge calculated the distance by bus between Mississippi and Illinois, then pronounced sentence: "You can stay with us for seven days." The hearing lasted less than ten minutes.

The airman spent a week in jail, every day in his dress uniform, since his duffle bag was confiscated. His jailers were polite, most likely because of the uniform. After asking repeatedly for several days, he found a jailer who would let him use a telephone. His family did not have a phone in their apartment on West 98th Street, so he called the janitor and left a message that he was not coming home, without revealing the circumstances. He saw a number of Black men brought to jail that week: some drunk, one badly beaten. He heard blues harmonizing and hollers, the *wooo* of a distant train spiraling from a human mouth. At six feet four inches, he splayed across his bunk, ambushed by the chill of Mississippi nights in December, becoming more furious every night. When he left Biloxi, headed for Illinois, he sat in the front of the bus again, this time without incident.

He says that the week of Christmas 1949 in Biloxi, Mississippi, was "wonderful." He says that he decided what to do with his life.

A man without religion, he experienced a different kind of epiphany. He did not glimpse an angel in the gleam of that flashlight. But, after this and other incidents, he was now intimate with the breath of racist encounters; at nineteen, he committed himself to resisting that bigotry. He was, to use his word, "primed" to join the civil rights movement. From that point forward, all his work, from community organizing to documentary photography, was anchored in opposition to racism.

Frank Espada, my father, never told me about Biloxi during my upbringing. When I was fifteen years old, I discovered a discarded page from his résumé which summarized the experience in a few terse sentences. Later, I would hear him tell the story to others; I had learned to be an expert eavesdropper around my father. The first time he ever told me the entire story directly was when I informed him that I was going to visit Biloxi, Mississippi, myself. I was forty years old.

A few years before this, I had written a poem called "Sleeping on the Bus." The third stanza refers to the Biloxi incident. My father is not named; rather, he is an anonymous "brown man" who "sneered at the custom of the back seat," meant to represent all the nameless people who sacrificed themselves to protest the laws of American apartheid. Even as I honor the act of resistance, I acknowledge in the poem that I do not fully appreciate that act: "and still I forget." The stanza is partly fictionalized: the judge "proclaimed a week in jail / and went back to bed with a shot of whiskey." The drama is deliberately intensified, for the sake of representing all such incidents through this single incident: "how the brownskinned soldier could not sleep / as he listened for the prowling of his jailers, / the muttering and cardplaying of the hangmen / they might become."

At times a poet resembles a bird, patching together the nest from string, the cellophane of cigarette packs, and other human artifacts. I borrowed the emotional state in these last few lines from *another* racial incident involving my father: his confrontation at a certain segregated lunch counter in San Antonio, a tale more familiar to me. He recalls leaving the scene after that incident and listening tensely for the footsteps of possible pursuers crunching the gravel in the parking lot.

I visited Biloxi in January 1998. Glimpsing the highway sign that read "Welcome to Mississippi" triggered a pulsation of dread. Even before I knew of my father's experience there, the Mississippi of my young imagination was an inferno. Here Emmett Till was murdered for insulting a white woman; NAACP leader Medgar Evers was assassinated; three civil rights workers were found buried in a dam, killed by the Klan with the collaboration of the local police. Phil Ochs sang of the cops in Mississippi: "Behind their broken badges / they are murderers and more." My father played that record over and over during my childhood years, and I never understood why.

~~~

Nearly fifty years later, Biloxi is now a casino town. Countless casinos line Highway 90 along the Gulf Coast: President Casino, Isle of Capri Casino, Imperial Palace Hotel and

Casino, Casino Magic Biloxi, Grand Casino Biloxi. A gargantuan sign on Highway 90 features a cackling pirate and his parrot advertising the Treasure Bay Casino. The casino boasts "a 400-foot authentic replica of an 18th century pirate ship, which hosts Scalawag's Show Bar, Laffitte's Gourmet Buffet ... the loosest slots on the coast, friendliest table in the South, full service poker rooms" and "dockside gaming 24 hours a day." The gamblers at Treasure Bay somehow see themselves as the robbers, and not the robbed.

The coastline glitters at night, pirate ship included. This is not the Mississippi of Robert Johnson, his "blues falling down like hail" on a 1937 recording that crackles like bacon frying. There are clues, however, that another Mississippi is not only present, but cherished.

In the midst of the casinos on the highway sits a white-pillared mansion called Beauvoir, the "Historic Last Home of Jefferson Davis." The President of the Confederacy is memorialized there by the "Jefferson Davis Shrine," presumably to facilitate the worship of Jefferson Davis. In the center of town, a dignified restaurant called Mary Mahoney's bills itself as "Old French House and Slave Quarters." The plaque on the wall of the eighteenth-century building refers to a "romantic past"; indeed, I was told that, until recently, the restaurant preferred to employ elderly Black men as waiters. This recalls a joke by an African-American comic whose name I have forgotten. He reports having had a cheery vacation at "Colonial Williamsburg," the reconstructed historical village in Virginia—until he was sold.

Upon entering the town, I encountered a bus station on Main Street, which, I had heard secondhand, was constructed in 1947. I paced between the diagonal yellow lines where the buses stop and wondered if Frank Espada had stepped across those same yellow lines.

When I entered the bus station, I was struck again by that pulsing dread. I drifted through the tiny depot, scanning the checkered floor, a stranger with no business there but the tracking of ghostly footprints. A clerk in a starched white shirt watched me from the ticket counter with seeming suspicion. I had always wondered what would happen to me if airport metal detectors could screen the gray baggage of my mind; now I wondered if the clerk could do the same.

I knew my reaction was irrational. The days of Jim Crow are over, and I am lightskinned anyway. This thought stumbled into another: my father is a different color. How could I possibly comprehend the experience of dark skin in Jim Crow Mississippi? How could I put my hand on that coarse texture? My father would describe the glower of white people in the South as "the Look." I remember, from adolescence, watching my father pay the tab at a seafood joint in rural Virginia while one of the poolplaying locals fixed him with the Look. But the Look was not for me.

Searching for any justification to remain in the bus station, I slipped a few quarters into a soda machine and bought an orange soda that I did not drink. I then dropped more change into a pay phone, and dialed a local number. I got the number wrong. When I walked outside the station and scratched in my notebook, the clerk strolled out with me. Maybe he thought I was the federal bus station inspector.

I had been attempting to call Deanna Newers, a Professor at Gulf Coast Community College and community historian who also worked at the Mardi Gras Museum in the Magnolia Hotel, which, the brochure said, "still possesses the aura of the Old South." I finally located Professor Newers at the Museum. While waiting for her, I drifted through the exhibits of mannequins in masks and capes, a collection of mutely strutting gargoyles. The mannequins were all white, as were all the faces in the vintage photographs on the wall. The brochure said that "The black community had their own parade." (No museum, though.) After reading a melodramatic tribute to the "Southern Gentleman" on the wall, I noted that the Mardi Gras King and Queen for 1949 were Howard McDonnell and Mary Rose Venus, respectively. The queen of the festival was officially dubbed "Queen Ixolib," which is Biloxi spelled backwards, like reading the word in a mirror. The Native Americans who involuntarily lent their name to this town might consider the inversion a telling commentary.

Professor Newers graciously guided me on a walking tour of the town. As we walked, she was able to point out the buildings that stood in 1949, and recall their demolished siblings. "Your father would have seen the Woolworth's over there," she said, or "your father would have seen the Masonic Temple here." I wanted to remind Deanna Newers that he was not in Biloxi on vacation in 1949, that there was no tour for him, that the Woolworth's would not have served him at the white lunch counter and the denizens of the Masonic Temple would not have ushered him into their secret society. I wanted to tell her to stop referring to my father as if he, too, were demolished brick, to tell her that he was a human being of almost seventy years with a diseased heart. But I wanted to match her graciousness, so I said nothing.

Finally, we arrived at the corner of Main Street and Howard Avenue. She informed me that the jail and municipal courthouse once stood here. We found ourselves in a parking lot. I was confronted with the startling fact that my place of pilgrimage was gone. While I was still working to assimilate that information, Professor Newers gestured across the street. We had circled back to the bus station where, she said, my father must have been arrested.

But that had to be wrong. My father clearly recalled being driven some distance in a police car from the bus station to the jail. If he had been arrested here, the police simply would have walked him across the street. Now nothing was certain. That procession of spectres, Frank Espada among them, was marching silently back into 1949 without a glance at me, as if that year were the foggy gulf and they were wading into its waters.

Then, at the Biloxi library, we encountered another community historian named Ray Bellande. Born in 1943, he recalled from childhood a Trailways station by the seawall, and offered to walk with me to the place where the station once stood. On the way, Ray Bellande endeavored to explain why my father was jailed in Biloxi. He squinted at me and said, slowly: "People had fewer personal freedoms back then." I yearned for a Distinguished Professor of Euphemism to translate the words "people" and "freedoms."

Rather predictably, a casino was being constructed on the spot where the Trailways station had been. This was Beau Rivage, or "Beautiful Shore," a huge, yellow, concrete and steel shell where cranes dangled like the fishing poles of a god lazily creating yet another world. Beau Rivage was owned by Golden Nugget Casinos of Las Vegas, and would open to the gamblers by the end of the year.

Wearily confusing my timelines, I visualized my father dealing blackjack at the Beau Rivage. Then I searched for him in the newspapers: the *Daily Herald* for December 1949, on microfilm at the library. Ray Bellande watched over my shoulder, reading me reading the microfilm, and repeating: "I don't think they would have reported this sort of thing."

They reported everything else. In the *Daily Herald* for December 24th, we read that judge J.D. Stennis fined John Michael Buren and Robert Harold Carter $10 apiece for disorderly conduct; fined Willie Parker, George Carlson, and Broker Huddleston $5 apiece for drunkenness; and fined Percy Case the sum of $1 for a parking violation.

Some of these men were probably my father's company in jail that week. Moreover, J.D. Stennis, whose name surfaces repeatedly in the *Daily Herald*, was certainly the judge who sent my father to jail. There was a Senator John Stennis who championed segregation in Congress for many years. It is not unreasonable to speculate that a Mississippi judge may have been kin to the Senator.

There was more news of crime in the *Daily Herald* from the week before Christmas 1949. Spec's Service Station was robbed, ten dollars in nickels taken from the cash register. A movie camera and binoculars were stolen from a car at the Hotel Biloxi. Police arrested an "armed negro" named Willie Richardson, who allegedly attempted to shoot "another negro," one Ernest Frank. Was Richardson the man my father saw in jail, badly beaten?

The newspaper reported other happenings in the "negro" community: the "Colored 4-H Banquet," the "Colored Toy Doll Fund Distribution," and "Colored Death." That was the headline for an obituary, as in, "Colored Death: Christopher Columbus Monroe, colored, a native of Alabama and a resident of Saucier for many years."

By bizarre coincidence, this was also the week that Joseph Stalin turned seventy, and every day the newspaper featured stories and columns such as, "Is Atheistic Communism Making a Deity of Stalin?" DeWitt MacKenzie opined that the answer was affirmative, and reasoned: "virtually all peoples, including primitive savages, believe in some kind of god." Apparently, the worship of Jefferson Davis was not considered primitive. There were also announcements of numerous Christmas parties and advertisements from local businesses proclaiming their belief in the Christian deity.

~~~

But Ray Bellande was right. The name of Frank Espada was nowhere mentioned in these pages. There was one more place to search for him: a law library back home, where I could research the legal history of segregation in public transportation. I am, after all, a lawyer, a fact I sometimes forget myself in this English-professor phase of my existence. At the law library, I made one final discovery: Frank Espada never broke the law at all.

In June 1946, three and a half years before the incident in Biloxi, the United States Supreme Court ruled in *Morgan v. Commonwealth of Virginia* (66 S.Ct. 1050) that state laws of segregation could not be applied to interstate bus travelers. Bus companies engaged in interstate travel could not segregate their passengers by color, and the driver could not compel a passenger to change seats because of color.

Irene Morgan, a Black woman traveling from Gloucester County, Virginia, to Baltimore, was arrested when she refused to sit in the back of the bus, and convicted of violating Section 4097d of the Virginia Code. She appealed, eventually to the Supreme Court. The argument ingeniously constructed by her attorneys, Thurgood Marshall and William Hastie, attacked the Virginia law as an "invalid burden on interstate commerce." They could not address the inherent injustice of de jure segregation in 1946 and win the case. The Court agreed with their argument, invoking the Commerce Clause of the U.S. Constitution.

Marshall and Hastie demonstrated that the application of local segregation laws to interstate buses—in ten different Southern states—was impractical, disruptive. Moreover, as the Court pointed out, the buses had "seats convenient for rest. On such interstate journeys the enforcement of the requirements for reseating would be disturbing." In other words, the driver might have to awaken a sleeping passenger; the Court envisioned the exact scenario in which my father found himself. This would be an "invalid burden on interstate commerce." The ironic fact that the Court decided the case on these narrow technical grounds, never directly challenging the system of racial segregation nor recognizing the deeper injury to Irene Morgan as a human being, illustrates why the Supreme Court is rarely a source of great literature or profound moral guidance.

According to Taylor Branch in *Parting the Waters*, his landmark study of the civil rights movement, the decision was not "widely enforced in the South." The Congress of Racial Equality sponsored a bus ride through the South in 1947, called the Journey of Reconciliation, to test enforcement of the new ruling. Branch relates that "white opponents met the challenge with beatings," and civil rights leader Bayard Rustin "was among those convicted under local segregation laws." In the midst of appeals, NAACP lawyers lost critical evidence: the interstate bus tickets. Rustin and his friends found themselves on a Southern chain gang. In 1963, my father would meet Bayard Rustin at the March on Washington; the following year, they worked closely together on a New York City public school boycott.

Throughout the South, state and local officials—governors, mayors, judges, and police—defied the Supreme Court and continued to implement segregation for another generation. An attorney at Greater Boston Legal Services, Jacqueline Bowman, once told me of a town in Tennessee where Blacks were still required to sit at the back of the bus in the 1970s, years after all segregation on public transportation had been outlawed. For every George Wallace, blocking the doorway to Black students and television cameras at the University of Alabama, there must have been legions of lesser officials throughout the hierarchy quietly, even surreptitiously, enforcing the same racial code.

In all probability, at least some of the actors in the Biloxi drama knew that Jim Crow could no longer reach into the door of that bus. It had been three and a half years since a police officer in Mississippi could legally arrest anyone refusing to sit at the back of a Trailways bus coming from or headed to another state; three and a half years since a judge in Mississippi could by law incarcerate an interstate bus traveler who refused to change seats because of color.

Perhaps the bus driver was unaware of changes in the law, and was simply acting to preserve the order of his tiny racial universe, at midnight, on an empty bus, as if shuffling the black and white pieces on a chessboard. On the other hand, Trailways drivers should have been informed by the company that they could no longer segregate their passengers on interstate trips; that may explain why the driver in San Antonio allowed my father to sit directly behind him.

What the arresting officers or jailers knew can never be proven. Yet, my father was not fingerprinted, photographed, or allowed a phone call when he was brought to the Biloxi jail, a shadowy scenario closer to an abduction than a legal arrest. The farther this case moved up the ladder of authority, the more likely it was that someone acted consciously to enforce a law that was no longer law. The Biloxi judge was part of a judiciary in the South that was acutely sensitive to the edicts of the Supreme Court on segregation, and resisted those edicts. His concern that my father not be reported AWOL may well have been born of a desire to avoid an Air Force inquiry into the airman's disappearance. From the bench, he scolded my father about his lack of respect for the law, in a backwater fiefdom where the Supreme Court had no jurisdiction.

Finally, the absence of a journalistic record is striking. In a small-town newspaper in which everything was reported, from one-dollar parking violations to the theft of nickels at the gas station, there was no report of this incident. An understanding between the authorities and the newspaper in Biloxi would hardly be unique.

Frank Espada did not know that the law had changed. He was aware that he might be subjected to the rules of segregation. Those rules usually required only "any appreciable Negro blood" to be invoked, and, as he put it, "I'd been called 'nigger' by the cops before." In his mind, he was engaged in an act of civil disobedience against an unjust law. When I told him about the *Morgan* case, that he had never violated the law, he said: "Then I was kidnapped."

Sitting in the law library, I became aware that I was moving in the rhythms of a strangely familiar ceremony. I was acting like a lawyer preparing the defense of a client. I was ready to argue Frank Espada's case before that judge in Mississippi half a century ago. I wanted to brandish my copy of *Morgan v. Commonwealth of Virginia* before the judge and demand the acquittal of the defendant.

The fact is that he probably would have been sent to jail anyway. I have argued before too many judges who were cleverly venomous, arrogant as petty aristocracy, or merely doltish. From my days representing indigent tenants in court, I remember one white-haired judge who would immediately award victory to the landlord if it were revealed that the tenant was receiving welfare, which the judge regarded as shameful. Another judge would hold hearings that consisted of one question: Does the tenant owe rent? The laws of rent withholding aside, this judge would instantly render judgment for the landlord, with the breezy advice to the tenant that he or she could appeal. Most vividly, I recall representing a prison inmate at a disciplinary hearing. The "judges" were two guards and a social worker. Moments before the hearing, as I reviewed my opening argument that the supposed offense was a physical impossibility, my dreadlocked client leaned across the table and whispered to me: "Now don't forget the appeal!" His instincts proved to be reliable.

So I cannot unscrew the jailhouse door from its hinges, nor make justice appear in my hands like a magician's dove.

What I found in Biloxi was the splintering of history. I unearthed a fragment, jagged and inscrutable as a shard of pottery or bone. But this fragment—my father's story—is evidence of how actual human beings behaved in the face of an enormous crime: the orchestration of a racial caste system with its roots in slavery. The crime is so vast that the scattered fragments of its history are buried everywhere, and everywhere the graves are unmarked.

Now Biloxi's history fossilizes beneath a proliferation of casinos. A casino is under construction at the place where my father was arrested; the parking lot where the jail and courthouse stood belongs to a corporation called Casino America. The casinos sprout along the coastline for economic reasons, not for the calculated interment of the past. But in their pseudo-elegance, their air of ersatz adventure, the casinos simultaneously evoke the shiny, prosperous image of the New South and the misty, romantic image of the Old South. Both myths demand that collective memory must plow the bodies of segregration and slavery deep into the ground. Certain histories have always been obliterated for the sake of commerce. And what better metaphor for the impulse to forget than the act of gambling, the vertigo of the roulette wheel? Everybody can play pirate.

⁓

The community historians want to preserve old Biloxi, conserve the old buildings in a historic district. Some of that knowledge is useful, and I am grateful for their cooperation, which would have been impossible in my father's Mississippi. But, for all their good will and good manners, they cannot seem to transcend the notion that history consists of minutiae in neutral colors, the what-was-where-when. This also constitutes a splintering of history. I think of wandering in the Mardi Gras Museum, in the palace of Queen Ixolib and her mannequin handmaidens, an empire where words are mirrored backwards and all the revelers are white. It is here that the front of the bus becomes the back of the bus.

The splintering of my father's history began at the instant of his arrest. By not taking his fingerprints, the police in effect wiped away their own. This is characteristic of splintered history: the fragments are scattered immediately in the sand, over time becoming driftwood, beach glass. Thus the perpetrators, the collaborators, the bystanders, the ambivalent, and the ignorant can all claim innocence for themselves and future generations: everyone is good.

On occasion, in a euphoria of alcohol and bloodlust, a lynching party and the witnesses to that killing would pose for the camera, smirking and pointing at the corpse in the trees. But soon after, the corpse was ash, the smirking mouths pursed in secrecy. Of course, my father was not lynched; but segregating the buses, or jailing someone for refusing segregation, falls somewhere along the same spectrum of terror and humiliation. Quotidian segregation could only be enforced by the constant threat of violence, and was itself a form of violence. In my poem, "Imagine the Angels of Bread," I envision a time when "darkskinned men / lynched a century ago / return to sip coffee quietly / with the apologizing descendants / of their executioners." During my time in Biloxi, no one I met expressed the slightest compassion or regret for what happened there to my father.

Yet, I have that fragment, an heirloom more prized than the family pocketwatch I lost twenty years ago. I can no longer rub the brick of jailhouse or bus station, but I still have words, my father's and mine. I write this account, and so build my father a museum of words, where a glass case displays the seat on the bus where he said "no."

I may build that museum more for myself than for him. I still want to read the walls, like a high school student on a field trip, and educate myself on the complex subject of my father. We were estranged once, not speaking for three years. At forty, I realize that we must speak while we still have the power of speech, that there will be millennia enough for silence.

At the end of my visit to Biloxi, I returned without my local guides to the parking lot at the corner of Main Street and Howard Avenue. *Here,* I said to myself, and carved my heel into the concrete and dirt. There was an epiphany on the bottom of my shoe.

I keep returning to one moment in Frank Espada's narrative. When my father left Biloxi for Illinois, after a week in jail, *he sat in the front of the bus.* He says today that he probably would have moved to the back if told to do so, that he was concerned about going AWOL. If that were the case, however, he could have sat in the back to begin with and eliminated the possibility of another arrest. What he did was dangerous: a second act of defiance could have provoked a far more hostile reaction than the vicious pettiness of that first confrontation. His uniform might not have shielded him from lethal consequences. Taylor Branch reports that Southern mobs "assassinated no fewer than six Negro war veterans in a single three week period" during the summer of 1946.

The second act of defiance was even more significant. This moment points like a storm-pounded weathervane in the direction of my father's political and ethical choices for the next fifty years. As a poet, I aspire to the grace and metaphor of that gesture; as a teacher, I aspire to the clarity and conviction of that gesture. I always will.

I am sending my father a postcard that reads "Greetings From Biloxi"—unless he holds it up to a mirror.

Argue Not Concerning God

I was raised by a Puerto Rican father and a Jewish-Jehovah's Witness mother. They met while working at the same factory in Brooklyn; my father was a shipping clerk, my mother a receptionist. Frank Espada was a skeptical, and wayward, Catholic. Marilyn Levine ate cheeseburgers and expected to be bug-zapped by God for mixing meat and milk, in violation of dietary laws.

There is a context for her repudiation of the Jewish faith and identity in favor of a relentlessly proselytizing door-to-door Christian sect most people find more irritating than a case of ringworm. Sometime between her marriage to my father in 1952 and my arrival in 1957, my mother's family disowned her. At age two, I glimpsed my mother's father, who escaped from a nursing home; in forty years, this is the only time I can remember meeting anyone on her side of the family, so complete was our ostracism.

Boxed into the Linden projects of East New York with three children in the early 1960s, my mother heeded a stranger at the door selling magazines and prophecy. During my father's regular absences, my siblings and I became, in effect, Witnesses as well. We learned that the Witnesses predicted "the end of this system of things," or Armageddon, a reference to the apocalypse, characterized in the magazines by pictures of crowds shrieking and cowering under a hail of fire. However, the Witnesses always chirped about "the good news" whenever they forecast the tongue-rotting demise of the damned (i.e. anyone not a Jehovah's Witness). After Armageddon came Paradise, like dessert.

Illustrations of Paradise featured somnambulent beneficiaries of eternal life petting equally stupefied lions: Jehovah as taxidermist. The gardens were sterile, the faces numb with narcotic smiles. The Witnesses equated perfection with the deliberately bland, even when they sang. At an early age, I was convinced that their hymns were based on theme songs from television shows. Their aversion to any exuberant or celebratory worship, their awkward austerity, also explain why the Witnesses do not observe Christmas. Of course, millions of people in the United States have no need for this particular holiday; but Christmas, or the lack thereof, became a metaphor for my family's contradictions and illusions.

～～～

We celebrated Christmas when I was very young. I can recall swatting my brother into the Christmas tree, which collapsed with the explosion of ornamental bulbs, a detonation of holiday grenades. My parents discovered me untangling my brother, and a great bellowing ensued. (I have learned since that other families also use their Christmas trees as projectiles. My father-in-law once heaved his Christmas tree like a harpoon through a picture window.)

Some time thereafter, my mother announced that she would no longer observe Christmas. She took the official Witness position that Jesus was not actually born on December 25th. This was an ancient Roman holiday—a pagan holiday. My father ruled in turn that, if my mother wouldn't celebrate Christmas, then nobody would. This was a family holiday, and if my mother wouldn't celebrate Christmas, then we wouldn't celebrate Christmas *together*, like a family.

However, my father kept his lifelong collection of Christmas ornaments, presumably hoping that my mother would change her mind. My mother made her state of mind very clear one December, a few days before Christmas, during my adolescence. She gathered my father's Christmas ornaments, dropped them in a garbage can, dragged the can to the corner, waited for the trashman to jingle the garbage into his truck, then returned to the house and declared to my father that she had thrown out his treasures.

She did it on his birthday. The Witnesses do not celebrate birthdays, either. This is considered self-exaltation, idol worship. For one day, you are the Golden Calf. Besides, the only two people to have birthday celebrations in the Bible are Pharoah and Herod. Following this logic, a few balloons and conical party hats may lead the birthday boy or girl to conquer vast deserts and dragoon thousands of slaves to build pyramids.

Thus my mother tossed Feliz Navidad into a trash compactor. The argument that followed combined the best features of a theological debate and a cockfight: God, Darwin, screeching, and feathers. I cannot recall my father's words. First his jaw trembled, which was always the prelude to a seismic event. Then the eruption began, his mouth open so wide I swore that I could see his uvula, that tiny punching bag, as if he were a cartoon opera singer.

One of my mother's most frequent quotations from the Bible comes to mind: Jesus said, "I came to put, not peace, but a sword" (Matthew 10:34). Jehovah's Witnesses would cite this verse to justify the breakup of families. Of course, this is the Witnesses' own "New World" translation of the Holy Scriptures. Considering the intricacies of translation from an ancient language, Jesus might well have said, "I came to poach a naughty piece of swordfish."

~~~

After my mother's Garbage Offensive, there was no talk of Christmas. My father bought me a duffle bag one Christmas. He told me: "Hey. I'm buying you a duffle bag." To which I replied: "I don't want a duffle bag." He responded: "You're getting a duffle bag." And so he gave me a duffle bag, unwrapped, so I would know that it was a duffle bag. Oddly enough, I was not planning on going anywhere.

In high school, I became a Christmas anarchist. I explained the fact that my family didn't celebrate Christmas in revolutionary terms. Christmas was a manifestation of corrupt consumer culture, a capitalist conspiracy, a hypocritical ceremony of the war-mongering state. Some of which is no doubt true, though what mattered was the marriage of convenient logic and high sanctimony. I was feeling very spiritual.

But I did not need the Witnesses anymore. My father's arguments for agnosticism and evolutionary theory were ultimately persuasive. My mother's only response to the theory of evolution was, "You may be descended from an ape, but I'm not." My mother's credibility also suffered when the Witnesses predicted "the end" for October 1975, and nothing ended but the baseball season. Moreover, in high school I had discovered girls. One cherubic creature from the local congregation left me with the demeanor of a cow brained by a sledgehammer. I became enamored of this particular headache, and, since the Witnesses dictated a code of sexual behavior only a Ken doll could obey, my choices were crystallized.

This is an account of redemption, however. My Christmas history was redeemed by pork: pernil in steaming chunks, with slivers of garlic, and cuero, the skin that cracked in my squeaking teeth. Every Christmas season, during our Brooklyn years, we would travel to the Bronx for dinner at my grandmother's apartment. I was buttoned into my blue suit, a diminutive pallbearer. I then drifted in a dramamine twilight as the car lumbered through traffic. The only mention of God was my father's litany of "Goddammit! Goddammit!" as we inched down the oxymoronic freeway. Once we arrived in the Bronx, my father would load me with presents for my cousins, and I reeled up five flights of tenement stairs. The door opened on what must have been thousands of Puerto Ricans, all related to me, and the slow dizzy bolero on the record player that left me swaying like a buoy at high tide.

Then came my grandmother's pernil, with arroz con gandules. A boy of generous girth is apt to believe that divinity is a plate of roast pork with rice and pigeon peas. This was the celestial feast. Mysteriously, my grandmother never ate. No one ever saw Tata chew or swallow anything. That was further evidence of the miraculous, a virtual weeping statue in the town plaza.

After dinner, my father would organize the family photograph, a gallery of faces with the broad Roig nose, my grandmother's nose and mine, a hill with two caves. My mother posed with the pagan Puerto Ricans, forgetting for the moment that Christmas was not the birthday of Jesus, ignoring the omnipresent plaster saints of the Bronx, simply because the pagans insisted on waving her into their snapshots.

My mother is still a Jehovah's Witness. Unlike me, my young son has never heard a debate over whether *his* father is descended from an ape. My wife, born on a Connecticut dairy farm, crafts ornaments by hand and saws down her own Christmas tree in the woods. We celebrate Hanukkah and the Día de Reyes, too. Expensive, true, but this year I am planning to moonlight as a professional wrestler to bring in some holiday cash—ring name *El Pernil.*

I leave the final word to that great Puerto Rican poet, Walt Whitman, from the 1855 introduction to *Leaves of Grass:* "This is what you shall do: Love the earth and the sun and the animals, despise riches, give alms to every one that asks, stand up for the stupid and crazy, devote your income and labor to others, hate tyrants, argue not concerning God...."

The Puerto Rican Dummy
and the Merciful Son

~~~

I have a six-year-old son, named Clemente. He is not named for Roberto Clemente, the baseball player, as many are quick to guess, but rather for a Puerto Rican poet. His name, in translation, means "merciful." Like the cheetah, he can reach speeds of up to sixty miles an hour. He is also, demographically speaking, a Latino male, a "macho" for the twenty-first century.

Several years ago, we were watching television together when a ventriloquist appeared with his dummy. The ventriloquist was Anglo; the dummy was a Latino male, Puerto Rican in fact, like me, like my son. Complete with pencil mustache, greased hair, and jawbreaking Spanish accent, the dummy acted out an Anglo fantasy for an Anglo crowd that roared its approval. My son was transfixed; he did not recognize the character onscreen, because he knows no one who fits that description, but he sensed my discomfort. Too late, I changed the channel. The next morning, my son watched Luis and María on *Sesame Street,* but this was inadequate compensation. *Sesame Street* is the only barrio on television, the only neighborhood on mainstream television where Latino families live and work, but the comedians are everywhere, with that frat-boy sneer, and so are the crowds.

However, I cannot simply switch off the comedians, or explain them (how do you explain to a small boy that a crowd of strangers is angrily laughing at the idea of *him?*). We live in Western Massachusetts, not far from Springfield and Holyoke, hardscrabble small cities which, in the last generation, have witnessed a huge influx of Puerto Ricans, now constituting some of the poorest Puerto Rican communities in the country. The evening news from Springfield features what I call "the Puerto Rican minute." This is the one minute of the newscast where we see the faces of Puerto Rican men, the mug shot or the arraignment in court or witnesses pointing to the bloodstained sidewalk, while the newscaster solemnly intones the mantra of gangs, drugs, jail. The notion of spending the Puerto Rican minute on a teacher or a health care worker or an artist in the community apparently never occurs to the producers of this programming.

The Latino male is the bogeyman of the Pioneer Valley, which includes the area where we live. Not long ago, there was a rumor circulating in the atmosphere that Latino gangs would be prowling the streets on Halloween, shooting anyone in costume. My wife Katherine reports that one Anglo citizen at the local swimming pool (a veritable Paul Revere in swim trunks) took responsibility for warning everyone that "the Latinos are going to kill kids on Halloween!" Note how 1) Latino gangs became "Latinos" and 2) Latinos and "kids" became mutually exclusive categories.

My wife wondered if this warning contemplated the Latino males in her life, if this racially paranoid imagination included visions of her professor husband and his toddling offspring as gunslingers in full macho swagger, hunting for "gringos" in Halloween costumes. The rumor, needless to say, was unfounded.

Then there is the national political climate. In 1995, we saw the spectacle of a politician, California Governor Pete Wilson, being seriously considered for the presidency on the strength of his support for Proposition 187, the most blatantly anti-Latino, anti-immigrant initiative in recent memory. There is no guarantee, as my son grows older, that this political pendulum will swing back to the left; if anything, the pendulum may well swing further to the right. That means more fear and fury and bitter laughter.

~~~

Into this world enters Clemente, which raises certain questions: How do I think of my son as a Latino male? How do I teach him to disappoint and disorient the bigots everywhere around him, all of whom have bought tickets to see the macho pantomime? At the same time, how do I teach him to inoculate himself against the very real diseases of violence and sexism and homophobia infecting our community? How do I teach Clemente to be Clemente?

My son's identity as a Puerto Rican male has already been defined by a number of experiences I did not have at so early an age. He has already spent time in Puerto Rico, whereas I did not visit the island until I was ten years old. From the time he was a few months old, he has witnessed his Puerto Rican father engaged in the decidedly non-stereotypical business of giving poetry readings. We savor

new Spanish words together the same way we devour man-
goes together, knowing the same tartness and succulence.

And yet, that same identity will be shaped by negative
as well as positive experiences. The ventriloquist and his
Puerto Rican dummy offered Clemente a glimpse of his inevitable future: Not only bigotry, but his growing awareness
of that bigotry, his realization that some people have con-
tempt for him because he is Puerto Rican. Here his sense of
maleness will come into play, because he must learn to deal
with his own rage, his inability to extinguish the source of
his torment.

～～

By adolescence, I had learned to internalize my rage. I
learned to do this in response to a growing awareness of
bigotry, having left my Brooklyn birthplace for the town of
Valley Stream, Long Island, where I was dubbed a spic. To
defend myself against a few people would have been feasi-
ble; to defend myself against dozens and dozens of people
deeply in love with their own racism was a practical impossibility. So I told no one, no parent or counselor or teacher
or friend, about the constant racial hostility. Instead, I
punched a lamp, not once but twice, and watched the blood
ooze between my knuckles, as if somehow I could leach the
poison from my body. My evolving manhood was defined by
how well I could take punishment, and paradoxically I pun-
ished myself for not being man enough to end my own humiliation. Later in life, I would emulate my father, and rage
openly. Rarely, however, was the real enemy within earshot,
or even visible.

Someday, my son will be called a spic for the first time;
this is as much a part of the Puerto Rican experience as the
music that inspires him to dance gleefully. I hope he will tell

me. I hope that I can help him handle the glowing toxic waste of his rage. I hope that I can explain clearly why there are those waiting for him to explode, to confirm their stereotypes of the hot-blooded, bad-tempered Latino male who has, without provocation, injured the Anglo innocents. His anger—and that anger must come—has to be controlled, directed, creatively channeled, articulated but not all-consuming, neither destructive nor self-destructive. I keep it between the covers of the books I write.

The anger will continue to manifest itself as he matures and discovers the utter resourcefulness of bigotry, the ability of racism to change shape and survive all attempts to snuff it out. "Spic" is a crude expression of certain sentiments that become subtle and sophisticated and insidious at other levels. Speaking of crudity, I am reminded of a group organized by whites in Brooklyn during the 1960s under the acronym of SPONGE: the Society for the Prevention of the Niggers Getting Everything. When affirmative action is criticized today by Anglo politicians and pundits with exquisite diction and erudite vocabulary, that is still SPONGE. When and if my son is admitted to school or obtains a job by way of affirmative action, and is resented for it by his colleagues, that will be SPONGE, too.

Violence is the first cousin to rage. If learning to confront rage is an important element of developing Latino manhood, then the question of violence must be addressed with equal urgency. Violence is terribly seductive; all of us, especially males, are trained to gaze upon violence until it becomes beautiful. Beautiful violence is not only the way to victory for armies and football teams; this becomes the solution to everyday problems as well. For many characters on the movie or television screen, problems are solved by *shooting* them. This is certainly the most emphatic way to win an argument.

Katherine and I try to minimize the seductiveness of violence for Clemente. But his dinosaurs still eat each other, with great relish. His trains still crash, to their delight. He is experimenting with power and control, with action and reaction, which brings him to an imitation of violence. Needless to say, there is a vast difference between Stegosaurus and Desert Storm.

Again, all I can do is call upon my own experience as an example. I not only found violence seductive; at some point, I found myself enjoying it. I remember one brawl in Valley Stream when I snatched a chain away from an assailant, knocked him down, and needlessly lashed the chain across his knees as he lay sobbing in the street. That I was now the assailant with the chain did not occur to me.

I also remember the day I stopped enjoying the act of fistfighting. I was working as a bouncer in a bar, and found myself struggling with a man who was so drunk that he appeared numb to the blows bouncing off his cranium. Suddenly, I heard my fist echo: *thok.* I was sickened by the sound. Later, I learned that I had broken my right ring finger with that punch, but all I could recall was the headache I must have caused him. I never had a fistfight again.

Parenthetically, that job ended another romance: the one with alcohol. Too much of my job consisted of ministering to people who had passed out at the bar, finding their hats and coats, calling a cab, dragging them in their stupor down the stairs. Years later, I channeled those instincts cultivated as bouncer into my work as a legal services lawyer, representing Latino tenants, finding landlords who "forgot" to heat buildings in winter or exterminate rats to be more deserving targets of my wrath. Eventually, I even left the law.

Will I urge my son to be a pacifist, thereby gutting one of the foundations of traditional manhood, the pleasure taken in violence and the power derived from it? That is an ideal state. I hope that he lives a life which permits him pacifism. I hope that the world around him evolves in such a way that pacifism is a viable choice. Still, I would not deny him the option of physical self-defense. I would not deny him, on philosophical grounds, the right to resistance in any form that resistance must take to be effective. Nor would I have him deny that right to others, with the luxury of distance. Too many people in this world still need a revolution.

When he is old enough, Clemente and I will talk about matters of justification, which must be carefully and narrowly defined. He must understand that abstractions like "respect" and "honor" are not reasons to fight in the street, and abstractions like "patriotism" and "country" are not reasons to fight on the battlefield. He must understand that violence against women is not acceptable, a message which will have to be somehow repeated every time another movie trailer blazes the art of misogyny across his subconscious mind. Rather than sloganeering, however, the best way I can communicate that message is by the way I treat his mother. How else will he know that jealousy is not love, that a lover is not property?

Knowing Katherine introduced me to a new awareness of compassion and intimacy, domestic violence and recovery. Her history of savage physical abuse as a child—in a Connecticut farming community—compelled me to consider what it means to heal another human being, or to help that human being heal herself. What small gestures begin to re-store humanity?

When the Leather
is a Whip

At night,
with my wife
sitting on the bed,
I turn from her
to unbuckle
my belt
so she won't see
her father
unbuckling
his belt

Clemente was born on December 28, 1991. This was a difficult birth. Katherine's coccyx, or tailbone, broken in childhood, would break again during delivery. Yet, only with the birth could we move from gesture to fulfillment, from generous moments to real giving. The extraordinary healing which took place was not only physical, but emotional and spiritual as well. After years of constant pain, her coccyx bone set properly, as if a living metaphor for the new oppor-tunity represented by the birth of this child.

White Birch

Two decades ago rye whiskey
scalded your father's throat,
stinking from the mouth
as he stamped his shoe
in the groove between your hips,
dizzy flailing cartwheel down the stairs.
The tail of your spine split,
became a scraping hook.
For twenty years a fire raced
across the boughs of your bones,
his drunken mouth a movie
flashing with every stabbed gesture.

Now the white room of birth is throbbing:
the numbers palpitating red on the screen of machinery
tentacled to your arm; the oxygen mask wedged
in a wheeze on your face; the numbing medication
injected through the spine.
The boy was snagged on that spiraling bone.
Medical fingers prodded your raw pink center
while you stared at a horizon of water
no one else could see, creatures leaping silver
with tails that slashed the air
like your agonized tongue.

You were born in the river valley,
hard green checkerboard of farms,
a town of white birches
and a churchyard from the workhorse time,

weathered headstones naming women
drained of blood with infants coiled inside
the caging hips, hymns swaying
as if lanterns over the mounded earth.

Then the white birch of your bones,
resilient and yielding, yielded again,
root snapped as the boy spilled out of you
into hands burst open by beckoning
and voices pouring praise like water,
two beings tangled in exhaustion,
blood-painted, but full of breath.

After a generation of burning
the hook unfurled in your body,
the crack in the bone dissolved:
One day you stood, expected again
the branch of nerves
fanning across your back to flame,
and felt only the grace of birches.

Obviously, my wife and son have changed me, have
even changed my poetry. This might be the first Puerto Rican poem swaying with white birch trees instead of coconut
palms. On the other hand, Katherine and I immediately set
about making this a Puerto Rican baby. I danced him to
sleep with roaring salsa. Katherine painted coquís—tiny
Puerto Rican frogs—on his pajamas. We spoon-fed him rice
and beans. He met his great-grandmother in Puerto Rico.

The behavior we collectively refer to as "macho" has deep
historical roots, but the trigger is often a profound insecu-

rity, a sense of being threatened. Clemente will be as secure as possible, and that security will stem in large part from self-knowledge. He will know the meaning of his name.

Clemente Soto Vélez was a great Puerto Rican poet, a fighter for the independence of Puerto Rico who spent years in prison as a result. He was also our good friend. The two Clementes met once, when the elder Clemente was eighty-seven years old, and the younger Clemente was nine months. Fittingly, it was Columbus Day, 1992, the 500th anniversary of the conquest. We passed the day with a man who devoted his life and his art to battling the very colonialism personified by Columbus. The two Clementes traced the topography of one another's faces. Even from his sickbed, the elder Clemente was gentle and generous. We took photographs, signed books. Clemente Soto Vélez died the following spring. My son still asks to see the framed photograph of the two Clementes, still asks about the man with the long white hair who gave him his name. This will be family legend, family ritual, the origins of the name explained in greater and greater detail as the years pass, a source of knowledge and power as meaningful as the Book of Genesis.

Thankfully, "Clemente" also has a literal meaning: merciful. Every time my son asks about his name, an opportunity presents itself to teach the power of mercy, the power of compassion. When Clemente, in later years, consciously acts out these qualities, he does so knowing that he is doing what his very name expects of him. His name gives him the beginnings of a moral code, a goal to which he can aspire. Merciful: Not the first word scrawled on the mental blackboard next to the phrase, "Puerto Rican male." Yet how appropriate, given that, for Katherine and me, the act of mercy has become an expression of gratitude for Clemente's existence.

Because Clemente Means Merciful

for Clemente Gilbert-Espada
February 1992

At three A.M., we watched
the emergency room doctor
press a thumb against your cheekbone
to bleach your eye with light.
The spinal fluid was clear, drained
from the hole in your back,
but the X-ray film
grew a stain on the lung,
explained the seizing cough,
the wailing heat of fever:
pneumonia at the age
of six weeks, a bedside vigil.
Your mother slept beside you,
the stitches of birth still burning.

When I asked, "Will he be OK?"
no one would answer: "Yes."
I closed my eyes and dreamed
my father dead, naked on a steel table
as I turned away. In the dream,
when I looked again,
my father had become my son.

So the hospital kept us: the oxygen mask,
a frayed wire taped to your toe
for reading the blood,
the medication forgotten from shift to shift,

a doctor bickering with radiology over the film,
the bald girl with a cancerous rib removed,
the pediatrician who never called, the yawning intern,
the hospital roommate's father
from Guatemala, ignored by the doctors
as if he had picked their morning coffee,
the checkmarks and initals at five a.m,
the pages of forms flipping like a deck of cards,
recordkeeping for the records office,
the lawyers and the morgue.

One day, while the laundry
in the basement hissed white sheets,
and sheets of paper documented dwindling breath,
you spat mucus, gulped air, and lived.
We listened to the bassoon of your lungs,
the cadenza of the next century, resonate.
The Guatemalan father
did not need a stethoscope to hear
the breathing, and he grinned.
I grinned too, and because Clemente
means merciful, stood beside the Guatemalteco,
repeating in Spanish everything
that was not said to him.

I know someday you'll stand beside
the Guatemalan fathers,
speak in the tongue
of all the shunned faces,
breathe in a music
we have never heard, and live
by the meaning of your name.

Inevitably, we try to envision the next century. Will there be a "men's movement" in twenty years, when my son is an adult? Will it someday alienate and exclude Clemente, the way it has alienated and excluded me? The counterculture can be as exclusive and elitist as the mainstream; to be kept out of both is a supreme frustration. I do not expect the men's movement to address its own racism in depth. The self-congratulatory tone of that movement drowns out any significant self-criticism. I only wish that the men's movement wouldn't be so proud of its own ignorance. The blatant expropriation of Native American symbols and rituals by certain factions of the movement leaves me with a twitch in my face. What should Puerto Rican men do in response to this colonizing definition of maleness, particularly considering the presence of our indigenous Taíno blood?

I remember watching one such men's movement ritual, on public television I believe, and becoming infuriated because the lead drummer couldn't keep a beat. I imagined myself cloistered in a tent with some Anglo accountant from the suburbs of New Jersey who was stripped to the waist and whacking a drum with no regard for rhythm, the difference being that I could hear Mongo Santamaría in my head, and he couldn't. I am torn between hoping that the men's movement reforms itself by the time my son reaches adulthood, or that it assimilates, its language going the way of Esperanto.

Another habit of language which I hope is extinct by the time Clemente reaches adulthood is the Anglo use of the term "macho." Before this term came into use to define sexism and violence, no particular ethnic or racial group was implicated by language itself. "Macho," especially as employed by Anglos, is a Spanish word that particularly seems to identify Latino male behavior as the very standard of sexism and violence. This connection, made by Anglos both intuitively and explicitly, then justifies a host of repressive measures against Latino males, as our presence on the honor roll of many a jail and prison will attest. Sometimes, of course, the perception of macho volatility turns deadly. I remember, at age fifteen, hearing about a friend of my father's, Martín "Tito" Pérez, who was "suicided" in a New York City jail cell. A grand jury determined that it is possible for a man to hang himself with his hands cuffed behind him.

While Latino male behavior is, indeed, all too often sexist and violent, Latino males in this country are in fact no worse in this regard than their Anglo counterparts. Arguably, European and European-American males have set the world standard for violence in the twentieth century, from the Holocaust to Hiroshima to Vietnam.

Yet, any assertiveness on the part of Latino males, especially any form of resistance to Anglo authority, is labeled "macho" and instantly discredited. I can recall one occasion, working for an "alternative" radio station in Wisconsin, when I became involved in a protest over the station's refusal to air a Spanish-language program for the local Chicano community. When a meeting was held to debate the issue, the protesters, myself included, became frustrated and staged a walkout. The meeting went on without us, and we later learned that we were defended, ironically enough, by someone who saw us as acting "macho." "It's their culture," this person explained apologetically to the gathered liberal intelligentsia. We got the program on the air.

I return, ultimately, to that ventriloquist and his Puerto Rican dummy, and I return too to the simple fact that my example as a father will have much to do with whether Clemente frustrates the worshippers of stereotype.

To begin with, my very presence—as an attentive father and husband—contradicts the stereotype. However, too many times in my life, I have been that Puerto Rican dummy, with someone else's voice coming out of my mouth, someone else's hand in my back making me flail my arms. I have read aloud a script of cruelty or rage, and swung wildly at imagined or distant enemies. I have satisfied audiences who expected the macho brute, who were thrilled when my shouting verified all their anthropological theories about my species. I served the purposes of those who would see the Puerto Rican species self-destruct, become as rare as the parrots of our own rain forest.

But, in recent years, I have betrayed my puppeteers and disappointed the crowd. When my new sister-in-law met me, she pouted that I did not look Puerto Rican. I was not as "scary" as she expected me to be; I did not roar and flail. When a teacher at a suburban school invited me to read there, and openly expressed the usual unspoken expectations, the following incident occurred, proving that sometimes a belly laugh is infinitely more revolutionary than the howl of outrage that would have left me pegged, yet again, as a snarling, stubborn "macho."

My Native Costume

When you come to visit,
said a teacher
from the suburban school,
don't forget to wear
your native costume.

But I'm a lawyer,
I said.
My native costume
is a pinstriped suit.

You know, the teacher said,
a Puerto Rican costume.

Like a guayabera?
The shirt? I said.
But it's February.

The children want to see
a native costume,
the teacher said.

So I went
to the suburban school,
embroidered guayabera
short-sleeved shirt
over a turtleneck,
and said, Look kids,
cultural adaptation.

The Puerto Rican dummy brought his own poems to
read today. *Claro que sí.* His son is always watching.

II. DISPATCHES

¿Viva Puerto Rico Gratis?

The Painful Patience of a Colony at the Close of the Twentieth Century

~~

Puerto Rico, as a colony in its centennial year under U.S. occupation, has a choice of battle cries: "Viva Puerto Rico Libre" or "Viva Puerto Rico Gratis." Both could be translated literally as "Long Live a Free Puerto Rico"—but such are the perils of translation. "Libre" means "free" in the sense of liberated, independent. "Gratis" means free of charge, for nothing, cheaper than the cheapest price. "Puerto Rico Libre" still exists as an ideal, a more widespread ideal than many realize, but "Puerto Rico Gratis" is a daily reality of colonized minds and colonized bodies, cheap labor, unemployment, dependence, and indignity. "Gratis" is the watchword of colonialism, for the right to self-determination itself has been given away. Still, the empty hands of a colony applaud on command, celebrating a foreign invasion that began in 1898 and has not ended yet.

I visited Puerto Rico with my wife and son in January 1997. We were in Viejo San Juan during the inauguration of re-elected pro-statehood Governor Pedro Rosselló, and the official celebration of the Día de Reyes—Three Kings Day—in the first week of January. We saw Puerto Rico Gratis.

In an apparent attempt to associate himself with the conquistadores who first plundered the island, the governor decided to deliver his inaugural address from El Morro. A huge platform with a podium rose before the old Spanish fortress like a Puerto Rican Trojan Horse.

The night before the governor's speech, I walked with a friend to the platform at the gates of El Morro. My friend is a painter with ties to the independence movement; her great amor will spend decades in federal prison for his part in another independentista "conspiracy." Though she is Spanish-dominant, my friend insisted on speaking English as we walked through El Morro. Puzzled, I switched back into Spanish several times, only to give up and finally speak English. I then noticed that the various police, security guards, and construction workers surrounding the governor's platform were allowing us to walk anywhere we wanted. We walked up to the platform and stood directly under the governor's podium. If we were the terrorists of FBI imagination, we could have left an incendiary bundle under that podium. But we were speaking English, so we could not possibly be terrorists, or independentistas, or Puerto Ricans. We were safe.

Governor Rosselló spent several million dollars on his own inauguration. My family and I stayed away from the speech, which created a crush of tailored dignitaries and aggravated the usual Viejo San Juan traffic. Instead, we wandered over to El Morro shortly after the inaugural address. The scene resembled a golpe de estado, the aftermath of a coup: the U.S. Army, the Puerto Rican National Guard, and the San Juan Police had conquered the environs of El Morro. There were helicopters slicing the air like monster dragonflies, mounted police wheeling their steeds into formation, and sidearms everywhere. The soldiers and police were not marching in a parade that afternoon. Many were watching, some casually, but watching. Perhaps they were watching for people with ideas like mine. Could they hear the whirring of my brain?

One young man in Army fatigues—a military policeman—grinned and saluted my camera. Emboldened, I asked another soldier if I could take his photograph. He nodded, leaning against a stone wall where two helmets rested like sleeping turtles. After I clicked the shutter, the soldier asked, unsmiling: "¿Es esta foto para *Claridad?*" He had been watching me as closely as I was watching him. "No, no, soy turista," I protested. In truth, while the photographs were not for the island's socialist newspaper, I had published poems in *Claridad,* and came close to telling him that. I left before the soldier decided he needed to keep my camera for security reasons. Maybe what had caught his attention was the small Puerto Rican flag painted on a fragment of coconut shell hanging around my neck; nowhere else but in a colony does a display of the national flag, without the flag of the colonizer, raise suspicions of subversive thinking. Someone later theorized that my beard was the problem, bushy and graying in the tradition of Fidel, which at least explains all those "random" searches by airport authorities.

The scene at El Morro that afternoon was like a dream induced by indigestion. Amid the infestation of Army, National Guard, and mounted police, there was a free carnival with clowns—inflated latex clowns. An enormous, disembodied clown head, purple and yellow, squatted before El Morro, strangely reminiscent of those ancient stone heads carved by the Olmec. Children dashed in and out of the clown's mouth. Parents lifted their flailing toddlers into the seats of demonstration jeeps and helicopters. Two other inflated latex clowns towered over the pandemonium, grinning blankly at the sight of the portable toilets along the wall of the nearby cemetery.

The Cementerio de San Juan abuts El Morro. Pedro Albizu Campos is entombed there. Yet the "apostle" of the independence movement, the leader of the Nationalist Party who spent nearly three decades imprisoned, is still locked up—when we attempted to visit his tomb, we found that the gate of the cemetery had been padlocked. If we could not visit the tomb, however, we could at least urinate in proximity to it. The portable toilets, khaki-colored, awaited us in soldierly rows.

The governor was gone. But he left his water behind. Rosselló's photograph appeared on small boxes of spring water, distributed for free. The legend at the top of the box read, "Compromiso Cumplido": "The Pledge Honored." The governor posed on the box in a dark suit, with a half-smile and his hands folded in front of him. The portrait radiated insincerity, the picture of a man asking us to trust him when his body language alone made clear that he could not be trusted. However, given his association with the conquistadores, the governor's intimacy with spring water made bizarre sense. Perhaps Governor Rosselló came to believe that he was Juan Ponce de León, the first governor of Puerto Rico, who died searching for the fountain of youth. Staring at the crumpled boxes strewn on the ground, I hallucinated the following poem:

The Governor of Puerto Rico Reveals at His Inaugural That He is the Reincarnation of Ponce de León

Marching through Florida in 1513,
Juan Ponce de León
smacked a mosquito against his neck
and cursed the fountain of youth.
His tongue was breaded with saliva;
cracks webbed his lips.
Ponce de León squinted at the sky,
remembering San Juan,
where as governor he could drowse
to the mating songs of frogs at dusk,
stroking his goatee
in contemplation of gold mines.
Again he smacked his welted neck
and tottered in his armor,
a tortoise straining to walk like a man.

Flash five centuries. The tongue
of Ponce de León is dust
behind a marble slab
in the cathedral of San Juan.
The elected governor of Puerto Rico

salutes the assembly at his inaugural,
as eight-ounce boxes of spring water
with the governor's picture
circulate through the crowd.
On the box, his posture is upright
with hands folded
like the high school principal of a nation.
At the gates of the conquistadores' fortress,
the governor announces
that he is the reincarnation
of Juan Ponce de León,
that he has dipped his smooth hands
in the fountain of youth at last, yes,
that all Puerto Ricans
will live forever
and always have rice and beans
if they drink the spring water
with his picture on the box.
"¡Brindis!" someone cries.
The crowd toasts the reincarnation
of the thirsty conquistador,
and everyone drinks the water
but the governor.

From the speech at El Morro to the face on the box of
spring water, from the mounted police to the flocks of helicopters, from the padlocked cemetery to the giant latex
clowns, this was both a manifestation of power and a par-
ody of power. This was force menacing and beneficent, the
genial patriarch on his day of triumph demonstrating his
charitable sensibility as well as his capacity to intimidate.
Yet this was farce, the chest-pounding of a colonial gover-

nor, pompous bravado from the elected leader of a nation with no control over whether that nation goes to war. If the U.S. Navy decided that El Morro would make a useful target for live bombardment in its war games—as the Navy decided about the offshore islands of Culebra and Vieques—then the governor would have to scurry for shelter with everyone else.

~~~

A few days later, the governor was no longer one of the conquistadores. He was now one of the Three Kings. The morning of January 6th began with a commotion beneath our balcony on the street called La Caleta de las Monjas. There was a National Guard tent across the street, where a banner announced: Abusar las Drogas es Abusar la Vida (To Abuse Drugs is to Abuse Life). The abuse of alcohol was not mentioned, a discreet gesture given the presence of the rum factory on the other side of the bay. Stamped on this banner warning of drug dependence—and emblazoned on the free, yellow National Guard balloons—was the logo of the National Guard: A Minuteman, symbol of the American Revolution, standing against the backdrop of the American flag.

We set off in search of the Three Kings. A sign directed the crowds to a "Gran Fiesta de Reyes—Hacia Paseo La Princesa." The sign was illustrated by a childlike drawing of the Kings. Beneath was a banner bearing the logo of the corporate sponsor for the Día de Reyes fiesta: Burger King. The banners for this monarchy of chopped beef tattooed the streets of the old city. Later, we saw Burger King himself, an actor in cape and crown hurrying through the cobblestoned streets, trailed by a pack of children who probably confused him with Baltasar.

Walking along the Paseo, we saw a towering inflated bottle of Pepsi; more Burger King banners; a gigantic, black and white fiberglass cow; a Salvation Army Emergency Disaster Services van giving out free cookies and juice; more scary giant latex clowns; a children's salsa band; a police salsa band, in khaki uniforms with saxophone, conga, güiro, sidearms, and seamless harmonies; a young man peering into a demonstration Army jeep as if he might volunteer the next day; and a bomb squad exhibit, featuring a dummy propped against a tree in a helmet and padded bomb squad gear. No Kings, though. In fact, the only physical evidence of the Reyes Magos we saw in Viejo San Juan that week was a live camel in a cage, under another parade balloon bottle of Pepsi, guarded by police who directed the file of camel-worshippers streaming past.

Our search for the Kings led us to the longest line of human beings I have ever seen. The line began at the edge of the Paseo fiesta, wound through the Plaza Colón onto Calle Fortaleza, past the Plaza de Armas to La Fortaleza, the Executive Mansion itself. *The San Juan Star* estimated, conservatively, that the line stretched for eight city blocks. This was the line to receive a free holiday gift from Governor Rosselló, First Lady Irma Margarita Nevares de Rosselló, and the Kings, all waiting in the interior courtyard of La Fortaleza.

The San Juan Star interviewed Gilberto Díaz of San Lorenzo, who arrived with his family at 6 a.m. and waited for five hours so his two-year-old daughter could receive a free Minnie Mouse doll. He expressed gratitude; the gift giveaway was "a big help, since I don't have a job." The *Star* reported this comment without irony. There is a direct connection, of course, between the policies of the governor—at the service of a ruling elite as well as the corporate interests

• of the colonizer—and the unemployment rate in Puerto Rico, which takes human shape in the face of Gilberto Díaz and his painful patience. Díaz was grateful for the free doll. In all likelihood, he would rather have a job.

The painful patience of Gilberto Díaz was reflected in every face on that line, which one police lieutenant estimated at more than 60,000. As we walked alongside the line for blocks, we heard virtually no arguments, no complaints, saw no shoving or jockeying for position. We also heard no laughter, saw almost no one grinning. There was no shade from the explosive sun. There was no food or water. There were no portable toilets. There was no music, until the last block. Vendors of piraguas pushed their carts down the line, but rarely sold their cups of fruit syrup and shaved ice. No matter how parched, this was a congregation without a dollar to spend for ice in the sun, which would only dissolve and be gone. A few dropped out of the line, sprawling in doorways with stunned eyes, sidewalk murals of defeat.

The government, with the duplicitous media, would have us believe that this spectacle of mass humiliation in fact represented an outpouring of popular affection for Rosselló and his party. This was a public relations smorgasbord. The gift giveaway was covered live on local television. Cheery TV reporters were careful to interview only those at the front of the line, finally about to pass through the gates of the Executive Mansion. Then the microphones turned to various government officials and members of the First Family who pronounced themselves pleased with their own benevolence. The next day, the *Star* reported the case of Verónica Cordero, who now had sixty-eight Barbies after her odyssey to La Fortaleza; the Barbies we saw, parenthetically, were all blonde, adopted by many a brown girl that

day. The *Star* also made this observation, with the rever- ·
ence of a celebrity-smitten tabloid: "Smartly dressed in dark
blue, the governor and his wife greeted everyone with a
smile and a warm greeting. Rosselló tended to ask the child
what kind of toy he or she wanted while his wife generally
held out a gift selected by one of her assistants." This brand
of reportage may explain why the *Star* is, as the masthead
proclaims, "The Only Pulitzer Prize-Winning Publication in
Puerto Rico."

Staggering back to our apartment, we watched more
pro-government jumping jacks on television. Brief profiles of
the governor announced that he held degrees from Harvard
and Yale. On occasion, the face of Pedro Rosselló would al-
ternate with the face of the First Lady, whose nickname,
Maga, sounded curiously like Mago. I had an epiphany. Al-
though Puerto Rico had become a laboratory for cultural
imperialism and political manipulation, at least I could still
name all Three Kings: Pedro, Maga, and Burger King.

Certainly, there were those standing in line who had voted
for Rosselló. There must have been those who wanted to
shake his hand. There were a few big blue styrofoam fingers
waving in the crowd, indicating support for the governor's
party. But the bankers and bureaucrats who supported
Rosselló were not standing in line. People do not stand in
line for five hours or more in the sun to walk away with a
free Barbie doll or Tonka truck if they can possibly do anything else. Here was a gathering of the working class and
the poor, carrying the crush of time on their shoulders like
any other fifty-pound sack, tragically patient with their rul-
ers, who promise jobs and distribute toys. So the colonized

are conditioned in obedience and dependency, shuffling forward for charity or warfare.

Still, I often hear this question from those unfamiliar with the Puerto Rican political landscape: Why do poor and working-class Puerto Ricans not vote for the pro-independence parties? The answer requires a historical context: namely, the repression of the independence movement in the twentieth century. Without some understanding of that repressive history and the fear it spawned—from the sedition trials and imprisonment of independentista leaders in 1936 and 1950, to the killings of independentistas by police at the Ponce Massacre in 1937 and Cerro Maravilla in 1978, to the harrassment and surveillance of independentistas today—the apparent alienation of the Puerto Rican majority from the option of independence is incomprehensible.

In this, the centennial year, an increasing number of Puerto Ricans in the United States express their support for independence. Statehood has not benefited the Puerto Ricans living in the states of New York, Illinois, or Massachusetts. Wounded by raw confrontations with racism, Puerto Ricans born or raised in the United States see a system unwilling to embrace either the barrio or the island itself. Should the mainland Puerto Rican community be allowed to vote in the next island plebiscite—as unlikely as that may be—the percentage for independence might be startling.

Meanwhile, the elite of Puerto Rico have mastered the art of manipulating the electorate to vote against its own interests, stirring up fear and anger and hope, giving away shiny trinkets in exchange for the treasure of the ballot. The irony is that the free toys aren't free at all. The militarized carnivals of the inauguration and Three Kings Day were exercises in distraction. With one hand the governor sows the crop of free toys; with the other hand he surrenders the economy, the workforce, the island's natural resources, and the right of self-determination to a colonial power.

~~~

That is Puerto Rico Gratis. Where is Puerto Rico Libre? Begin with history, the refusal of oblivion. In 1993, our compañero Clemente Soto Vélez—poet, independentista, political prisoner from 1936 to 1942—died and was buried in a grave unmarked but for a stick with a number and letter. When a small group of his friends, including my wife and I, discovered the grave in this condition of oblivion, we bought a gravestone and gave the poet his name back.

Now, leaving San Juan after the Día de Reyes, we drove into the mountain town of Barranquitas, where my grandfather, Francisco Espada Marrero, was born in 1890. He was eight years old at the time of the U.S. invasion. I never thought to ask him about the absurdities he may have witnessed. (The absurdities of conquest: I am reminded of the poet Carl Sandburg, who was then a youthful foot soldier from Illinois and part of the invasion force that landed in Puerto Rico. He was responsible for rowing his commander's dog ashore at Guánica.)

As I walked through the plaza of Barranquitas, I glimpsed a man approaching me who could have been my grandfather, now fifteen years dead. This man wore a white, wide-brimmed straw hat.

I expected him to do what my grandfather would do thirty years ago in Brooklyn: sit down on a bench, tug the creases of his pants, unfurl his brown, veined tobacco-leaf hands and say to me: "Vente." Come here. The man in Barranquitas never saw me, but I was replenished.

In nearby Aibonito, I met another man, Félix Rodríguez, who was a janitor in the same Manhattan office building for forty-five years. Finally, he retired to a small house in mountainous Aibonito, the coolest spot on the map of Puerto Rico, where there was a revelation: the man who cleaned floors for nearly half a century could make absolutely anything grow.

The Janitor's Garden

for Félix Rodríguez,
Aibonito, Puerto Rico, 1997

The office building at Forty-second and Lexington
sat awaiting the night janitor
like an executive anticipating a shoeshine:
sixty floors mopped and waxed every night,
five nights a week, fifty weeks a year,
for forty-five years: 675,000 floors gleaming.
The ammonia streamed its clear poison
in a cascade, as if from the temple of Ammon
in faraway Egypt, where ammonia began.

He inhaled the burning breath of ammonia
for half a century, and did not die.
He polished the floors for the polished shoes
of industrialists while they slept,
yet did not sleep with rum or wake in sweat.
He stacked the toilet paper of lawyers after midnight
as they stacked contracts and wills,
and did not quiver with desire for their paper.
The janitor kept his garden every night.

When the elevator doors opened
and his mop slid across the floor,
on that glistening spot an orange tree
would sprout, roots fingering through the tile.
A swipe of the mop
and another orange tree scraped the ceiling
with its unfolding fan of branches,
then again till the hallway
was an orange grove in bloom, brilliant
with the trees of China, as we say in Puerto Rico.
The scent of oranges banished ammonia,
and the cleaning crew dripped pulp and juice
to their elbows. Not one sneezed or coughed
in Manhattan slush, walking home after night shift.

On some mornings, a secretary would report
that the floors had been waxed with orange juice,
an errand boy might find peels floating
in all the toilets, or the day janitor discover
an orange in a paper bag scrawled with his name.
The lawyers snorted, blamed the menstrual cycle
or the imagination of colored people, then went to lunch.

Today Félix keeps his garden
in the hills of Aibonito. He is bald as an orange.
Without the ceiling pressing down
the trees become celestial jugglers
levitating orange planets. I climb to the roof
and soak my beard with luminous fruit
as he glances up from the garden,
leaning on his mop.

Like Félix Rodríguez—who literally refuses to drink the governor's water—the people of Puerto Rico still have creativity, resilience, and even a bit of subversive sorcery. There are those who believe that fighting for an independent Puerto Rico is like cultivating orange trees with a mop. Muy bién—pass the mop.

The New Bathroom Policy
at English High School

Dispatches from the Language Wars

~⌒~

My friend Jack Agüeros, a gifted Puerto Rican writer from East Harlem, explains his bilingualism with this analogy: "English and Spanish are like two dogs I love. English is an obedient dog. When I tell him to sit, he sits. Spanish is a disobedient dog. When I tell him to sit, he pees on the couch." Jack is articulating the difference in command between a first language and a second language. He has more control over English than Spanish. His command of Spanish is, in fact, more substantial than this modest analogy implies; his translation of Julia de Burgos, *Song of the Simple Truth*, was published by Curbstone Press in 1997.

As a Puerto Rican from Brooklyn, I also walk the obedient dog of English and the disobedient dog of Spanish. In the process, I have learned that the best way for me to maintain Spanish is to fight for the *right* to speak Spanish. Defending the right of all Latinos to use the tongue of their history and identity creates in me a passion for Spanish itself. Both as a lawyer and a poet, I have served as an advocate for Spanish, which is, ironically, my second language.

This kind of distinction, however, fades in the face of the cultural warfare which characterizes the United States today. There are too many in this country who would amputate the Spanish tongue. Given this cultural aggression, it is astonishing that more Latinos have not lost their Spanish altogether, that so many Latinos still speak as much Spanish as they do. Thus, under these circumstances, I write dispatches from the language wars of this América, in poetry and prose.

The hostility towards Spanish in the United States has been best documented by James Crawford, in works such as *Hold Your Tongue*, which chronicles the "English Only" movement. According to Crawford, this xenophobic movement is spearheaded by the organization called U.S. English, founded in 1983, which by the end of the 1980s had a budget of $7 million with a membership of 400,000. U.S. English devotes its energies to opposing bilingual education, ballots, government services, street signs, and 911 operators, as well as foreign-language broadcasting, the Yellow Pages in Spanish, and even a Spanish-language menu at McDonald's. Conversely, U.S. English lobbies to make English the official language at the state and federal levels. Its founder, John Tanton, was forced to resign after the leak of a blatantly racist anti-Latino memorandum warning that the Latino birthrate would consume Anglo America: "Perhaps this is the first instance in which those with their pants up are going to get caught by those with their pants down!"

~~~

The purists of English Only, and other linguistic zealots, believe that the English language is being corrupted from the bottom up: by "Spanglish," by "Ebonics," by all non-standard English as spoken by poor and working-class people. If anything, the English language is being eroded from the top down, by the dialects of the powerful: Legalese, medicalese, bureaucratese. These dialects seek to obscure, rather than clarify; their intent is not to communicate, but to control.

Of course, linguistic zealotry is not new. Theodore Roosevelt recommended early in this century that any immigrant who did not learn English within five years should be deported. Then there is the history of Puerto Rico under the United States: the notorious imposition of English on the schools and courts of the island represents a classic colonial use of language as an instrument of power.

The conflict became very tangible for me one morning in front of the Massachusetts State House in Boston. At the time, I was working for META, a non-profit, public-interest law firm specializing in bilingual education. META was involved in a demonstration on the steps of the State House, protesting a bill that had been introduced in the Massachusetts legislature to make English the official language of the state. The crowd sang and chanted in Spanish. I waited to speak to the crowd. Suddenly, I noticed a man racing down the steps of the State House, shouting at us. When I turned in the direction of the shouting, I found myself standing in his path. Reflexively, still thinking in Spanish, I said to him: "¿Cómo estas?" He squinted with rage, then threatened to rip my tongue out for talking to him in Spanish. He shoved past me and disappeared into the street.

Moments later, I found myself, microphone in hand, addressing the crowd. I was supposed to read poetry. Instead, still shaken, I spoke of the man who wanted to rip my tongue out because I greeted him in Spanish. "That's what they're trying to do to all of us," I said, then added: "He can rip my tongue out if he wants. But it won't work, porque yo hablo español con el corazón" ("because I speak Spanish with my heart"). The man who would rip out Spanish tongues was only expressing the same idea, in cruder form, as those legislators inside the State House who were attempting to make English the official language of Massachusetts, which would then serve as the foundation for legal discrimination against Spanish and against Latinos. They failed.

~~~

At META, we saw language discrimination cases on occasion. One case came from nearby Lynn, Massachusetts, where META represented the Hispanic Parent Advisory Council. A Latino parent called us and said: "Please come over to Lynn English High School. They have banned Spanish at lunchtime." The chief lunchroom aide overheard a few students speaking Spanish at lunch and concluded that they must be talking about the Anglos in their midst. The principal of the school supported her policy of prohibiting Spanish at lunchtime.

In a spasm of paranoia, many Anglos assume that the only reason Latinos speak Spanish in their presence is to say diabolical things about those same Anglos. This sometimes leads to the myopic declaration: "This is America! Speak English!" (The Chicano comic Paul Rodríguez has developed a clever twist on this kind of outburst. Faced with a similar situation on an elevator in Los Angeles, where several Chinese are speaking their native language in his presence, Rodríguez bellows: "This is America! Speak Spanish!")

I visited the school with fellow META attorney Camilo Pérez-Bustillo, and we held a hearing with the principal. He changed the policy. But one of the benefits of being a poet is the opportunity for revenge.

The New Bathroom Policy
at English High School

The boys chatter Spanish
in the bathroom
while the principal
listens from his stall

The only word he recognizes
is his own name
and this constipates him

So he decides
to ban Spanish
in the bathrooms
Now he can relax

A Puerto Rican hospital administrator in Connecticut told me that he read this poem aloud at a meeting, causing the hospital to reverse its policy of forbidding patients to speak Spanish among themselves.

If this hostile "English Only" climate sometimes breeds ab-
surdity, then it also breeds tragedy: in Lowell, Massachusetts, in 1987, a Cambodian schoolboy was drowned by his
white counterpart during a citywide battle over desegrega-
tion and bilingual education. Yet, according to Pérez-
Bustillo, "In more than fifteen years of working with
bilingual education programs, parents and students, I have
never met a single person who didn't want to learn English.
What they want to do is also retain their own language, culture, and identity."

After META, I worked for Su Clínica Legal, defending
the interests of indigent, Spanish-speaking tenants in Chelsea District Court, and training students from Suffolk University Law School in Boston to do the same. I witnessed in
court the association of the Spanish language with sloth,
deceit, ignorance, even savagery. Often, I found myself serving not only as attorney, but as translator. There was a
chronic shortage of court interpreters—our motions for interpreter services were routinely ignored—and if an interpreter was available, he or she was assigned to the criminal
court, since jailing Latinos was a higher priority than evicting Latinos. Under the best of circumstances, the language
of the law has great power to disorient its victims, even
those who are well-educated. That disorientation becomes
absolute dizziness, then, for those victims of the court system twice removed from legal language because of their inability to speak English. The results can be devastating. On
one occasion, I stepped forward in court to interpret for a
woman who was not my client.

Offerings to an Ulcerated God

"Mrs. López refuses to pay rent,
and we want her out,"
the landlord's lawyer said,
tugging at his law school ring.
The judge called for an interpreter,
but all the interpreters were gone,
trafficking in Spanish
at the criminal session
on the second floor.

A volunteer stood up in the gallery.
Mrs. López showed the interpreter
a poker hand of snapshots,
the rat curled in a glue trap
next to the refrigerator,
the water frozen in the toilet,
a door without a doorknob.
(No rent for this. I know the law
and I want to speak,
she whispered to the interpreter.)

"Tell her she has to pay
and she has ten days to get out,"
the judge commanded, rose
so the rest of the courtroom rose
and left the bench. Suddenly
the courtroom clattered
with the end of business:
the clerk of the court

gathered her files
and the bailiff went to lunch.
Mrs. López stood before the bench,
still holding up her fan of snapshots
like an offering this ulcerated god
refused to taste,
while the interpreter
felt the burning
bubble in his throat
as he slowly turned to face her.

~×~

Since leaving the law, my involvement in the community
has increasingly taken the form of bilingual poetry readings
and workshops, with barrio groups ranging from new immigrants to young Latinos who have never visited the home-
land of their ancestors. Though most are at least somewhat
bilingual, this is a community divided from itself by language, a consequence of cultural aggression. This division
was most dramatically illustrated for me by a reading at the
Care Center, a high school equivalency program for adolescent mothers in Holyoke, Massachusetts. Almost all the
young women were Puerto Rican: roughly half, the new ar-
rivals, spoke little English; the other half, born in Holyoke,
spoke little Spanish. I became a code-switching ping-pong
ball, every word repeated in both languages, so I could
reach all the Puerto Ricans in the room.

　　Yet, no matter which language I use as a poet, I could
not communicate with barrio audiences if my poems were
about vacations in Paris or nostalgia for an Ivy League education. Because the choice of Spanish is necessary, but not
sufficient. There must also be *subject*, and that subject
must reflect the experience of that community if I hope to

communicate. Some call that political poetry. Yet art is not sacrificed here. The Latino community is a worthy subject for art. The defense of the right to a Latino identity and the Spanish language is also the stuff of poetry.

This is especially true in the age of Proposition 187. Approved by referendum in California and now snarled in litigation, Proposition 187 would prevent immigrants from receiving basic human services, such as education and health care. Behind 187 lurks the fear of Latinos and their language, reflected everywhere from electoral politics to pop culture. Governor Pete Wilson of California became the most visible and vociferous proponent of 187.

Governor Wilson of California Talks in His Sleep

The only
aliens
we like
are the ones
on *Star Trek*,

'cause
they all
speak
English

Living in the United States, one becomes aware of the popular belief that English is the only language spoken in the universe, a notion reinforced by the English-speaking aliens of *Star Trek*. My wife, who teaches sociology at Springfield Technical Community College, encountered one student who insisted that English should be the only language spoken in this country "because the Bible was originally written in English." This ignorance is sometimes manifested in simple ways, such as the stubbornly persistent mispronounciation and misspelling of Spanish names. So it is that Mr. Espada may become Mr. Espalda, Mr. Esperanza, Mr. Empanada, etc. I once visited a classroom in Boston where I met a young man named Joaquin, whom his teacher introduced to me as "Joe Quinn." And the dropout rates continue to soar.

The repression of Spanish is part of a larger attempt to silence Latinos, and, like the crazy uncle at the family dinner table yelling about independence or socialism, we must refuse to be silenced. On October 12, 1996—Columbus Day—I gave a reading at a bookstore in Tucson, Arizona. The reading was co-sponsored by Derechos Humanos, a group which monitors human rights abuses on the Arizona-México border, and was coordinated with the Latino March on Washington that same day. Arizona is a state with a rapidly growing racist militia movement, a state where English is the official language by amendment (which has also been challenged in court and remains in limbo). At 7 p.m., the precise time when the reading was to begin, we received a bomb threat. The police arrived with bomb-sniffing dogs and sealed off the building. I did the reading in the parking lot, under a streetlamp. This is one of the poems I read that night, based on an actual exchange in a Boston courtroom:

Mariano Explains Yanqui Colonialism to Judge Collings

Judge: Does the prisoner understand his rights?
Interpreter: ¿Entiende usted sus derechos?
Prisoner: ¡Pa'l carajo!
Interpreter: Yes.

Multiculturalism
in the Year of Columbus
and Rodney King

~~~

Few words of recent coinage in our contemporary vocabulary are so praised and damned, so powerful yet misunderstood, as "multiculturalism." In 1992, this perspective challenged one event—the celebration of Columbus and the 500th anniversary of his encounter with the New World—and faced a challenge from another: the Los Angeles riots which followed the acquittal of the police officers who brutalized African-American motorist Rodney King. In the whirlpool of these struggles, we must stop swirling long enough to question and commit. The invigorated principle of multiculturalism becomes essential.

At its best, multiculturalism is not only an *approach*, but also a *movement*, with an impact on many realms of life: literature, the arts, social science, education, politics. The multicultural viewpoint recognizes that this society is

pluralistic, not monocultural, that we cannot all be meas-
ured by the same narrowly elite experience, a yardstick that
would have a few of us sharply dressed and most of us
wearing suits with sleeves that slap us and cuffs that trip us.

Progressive multiculturalism rejects the assimilationist
model for society, one that insists on unity through the sur-
render of identity, that perpetuates the romantic fiction of a
past when the nation was one with itself. A multicultural
perspective transcends mere "tolerance" of diversity—an
odd choice of words, given that "tolerance" implies a barely
repressed repugnance—and instead revels in that diversity.

Multiculturalism as a way of critical seeing explodes
the myth of meritocracy, focusing on the reality that no institution, no matter how intellectually or artistically en-
dowed, is immune from the social forces that surround it,
and that therefore the liberal arts college as well as the erudite
literary magazine may have to confront their own bigotries.

Multiculturalism ideally expresses the potential for
solidarity between very different groups of people who share
in common their marginality and the need to move from the
margin to the rest of the page. Multiculturalism is thus
driven by a democratizing impulse, which is by nature in-
clusive, embracing not only people of color, but broadening
to include a spectrum of cultures: other ethnic groups, gays
and lesbians, and so on. The literatures of these diverse
people then cross-pollinate. Sheila Packa, a poet I read with
in Saint Paul, Minnesota, was inspired to use the Finnish
language of her ancestors in her poems after reading the bilingual (Spanish-English) poetry of Puerto Rican Víctor
Hernández Cruz.

In its most progressive form, multiculturalism is about
change. Eduardo Galeano writes for "those who have been
standing on line for centuries to get into history." Viewed

from the perspective of centuries, the demands of multiculturalism are reasonable indeed. But demands they remain: for new pedagogy, new books, new analysis of racial dynamics, new cultural values, new history, and new opportunity. And demands they must be. Frederick Douglass understood this when he said: "Power concedes nothing without a demand. It never did, and it never will." If words and ideas matter—and those in power are well aware that words and ideas matter—then multiculturalism matters, which serves to explain in part the right-wing backlash against the movement.

~~~

Multicultural perspectives have been criticized as "political correctness," either trivialized as a new set of manners and mores designed not to offend, or demonized as the New McCarthyism, a wave of censorship soaking the nation's campuses in silence. This is the stuff of *Time* magazine, making its millions by scaring the middle class, which is cowed into believing that the tuition paid on behalf of its sons and daughters is diverted to courses on Swahili rather than Shakespeare, or worse, Shakespeare in Swahili. A false dichotomy is created between diversity and quality.

Dealing with the avalanche of criticism becomes overwhelming for the advocates of multiculturalism. People who have never read a book based on this approach have heard of multiculturalism and its evil twin, political correctness, and have been led to believe that this is indeed the New McCarthyism, the most insidious charge of all. Yet, as Camilo Pérez-Bustillo puts it: "Name one person whose life was ruined by multiculturalism. Name one person who has gone to jail. Name one person put on a blacklist, who had to write under a pseudonym. Name one person who could not leave the country, or who could not return, because of multiculturalism." Even the term "political correctness" is a misnomer, for what could be more politically correct than holding political power, or identifying with those who do?

The conservative criticism of the multiculturalist movement takes on an almost hallucinogenic quality. The marrow of multiculturalism is dissent, and yet this dissent supposedly stifles dissent. The call for debate is heard as a cry for censorship. An institution or individual confronted with a charge of racism may well be smothered in sympathy. Hang a Confederate flag from a Harvard dorm window, as one student did, to become a courageous defender of the First Amendment (which never applied to the slaves laboring beneath the Stars and Bars). The racist substance of what is said is never examined in the rush to defend the right to say it. The assumption here: It is worse to be called a racist than to actually be one.

The backlash exists for a multiplicity of reasons. The paranoia of the powerful is a factor. In a right-wing age, multiculturalism is that rare progressive movement which appears all the more threatening due to the vacuum which surrounds it. Though, in absolute terms, its impact is still modest—hardly in control of the cafeteria, much less the campus—there is more multicultural activity, involving a broader spectrum of people, on campuses and elsewhere, than ever, offending the guardians of the status quo. This increased presence also implies a new accountability: People of color, for example, are less likely to countenance blatant prejudice or discrimination than before.

There is also the deniability factor. U.S. educational and political systems have always denied the history and literature of those outside the narrow mainstream, especially with respect to race, the way a family might deny its own darkest sibling. In general, there is the usual head-banging struggle against change. Johnnetta Cole, an African-American administrator charged with curriculum reform at the University of Massachusetts, and now the head of Spelman College, commented that, "to ask a faculty to change its curriculum is like asking someone to move a graveyard."

Certain writers of color have calculated the profit of being right-wing in a right-wing age, and have peeled off their skin in a striptease for the applause of white politicians and academics who two centuries ago would have rationalized their enslavement. Thus, these sages condemn bilingual education, reject affirmative action, or rail against multiculturalism on campus, all apparently indifferent to being wielded as weapons against their own communities.

~~~

Yet, the movement for multiculturalism launched a serious challenge to a historical icon in 1992: Christopher Columbus. Even those defenders of the admiral who shook with indignation at the egging of their hero had to admit that the vandals were at the gates, smacking Columbus with the occasional egg fastball. This admission was itself a victory of sorts; the multicultural perspective was irrevocably part of the debate. Consider this: The left had a far greater impact on the Columbus debate than on the debate over the war with Iraq.

The salvo against Columbus was multiculturalism at its source. How can we respect African-American and Native-American people without recognizing their history of slavery and genocide in the Americas, as it began 500 years ago? We cannot respect that history, and kowtow to Columbus too. The defenders of Columbus argued that the benefits of the conquest outweighed the costs. But slavery and genocide cannot be so weighed. The scale breaks.

Others argued that Columbus must be separated from the historical consequences of his actions, which were unintended and unforeseeable, a chain reaction over which he had no control. This argument was demolished by books such as *The Conquest of Paradise* by Kirkpatrick Sale. Here we find Columbus the slaver, who first ordered "seven head" of indigenous people kidnapped and brought to his ship, then enslaved thousands of others; Columbus the plunderer, so obsessed with gold that he referred to the precious metal more than 180 times in the journal for the first voyage; and Columbus the tyrant, who, as governor of Española in 1495, initiated a tribute system whereby "Indians" brought gold dust to the Spanish, or had their hands cut off. During his administration, indigenous people were hanged by the Spanish in groups of thirteen, in honor of Christ and the Twelve Apostles.

If the movement for multiculturalism often finds itself doing battle over curriculum, even at the grade-school level, then the battle over Columbus was no different. I recently found a book about Columbus at a daycare center, with a cover depicting the admiral trading beads for parrots with the "Indians," leaving the impression that the conquest was a combination craft fair and exotic bird show. Left unsaid: that the indigenous population of Española evaporated in the steam of its own blood, "*from eight million to twenty-eight thousand in just over twenty years,*" according to Sale (his italics).

The only inheritance of the conquest worth saving is multicultural. The historian Hans Koning points out the creation of a new people in Latin America: "That race, as it now exists, of mixed Spanish and Indian and African stock....

These children of conquerors and slaves are the only achievement of the conquest, the only wealth it produced."

And Columbus? He will continue to be lauded as what Nancy Murray calls "the first European immigrant," the first pioneer, the first entrepreneur, confirming "self-celebratory myths" about this America. Thus the Knights of Columbus, defending the icon, condemned all criticism of the admiral as "neo-Marxist." But the Knights were too late. Eduardo Galeano saw the anniversary as an opportunity: "Not to confirm the world ... but to denounce and change it. For that we shall have to celebrate the vanquished, not the victors." The advocates of multiculturalism seized this opportunity, ranging in 1992 from a huge gathering of Native-American writers in Norman, Oklahoma, to a camp of Latino poets, artists, and musicians assembled at Columbus, New Mexico—the site of Pancho Villa's famous raid—to a small cultural event in Worcester, Massachusetts, where I read with African-American, Lebanese, and Abenaki Indian poets, all against Columbus.

The racism espoused by Columbus to justify conquest, slavery, and plunder is still with us. The swords used to slash Taínos who had never seen steel have become billy clubs. Those billy clubs battered Rodney King relentlessly after the African-American motorist was stopped by police in Los Angeles for a traffic violation. The notorious videotape was not enough for a jury that believed in the gospel of racism with more fervor than they believed in their own sense of sight. This was too much for los olvidados, the forgotten ones of that city, and their combustible rage exploded. Even the victims of the legal system must believe that the courtroom is just. When that illusion disappears, then only the stink of gasoline is left in the air.

If the demystification of Columbus in 1992 meant progress for the forces of subversive multiculturalism, then the Rodney King affair and the Los Angeles riots presented major challenges. How relevant is a multicultural curriculum at the moment that Rodney King bleeds on asphalt, symbolizing the power of the state to enforce racism through legalized violence? What impact could multiculturalism possibly have on the rioters, who had nothing, and now have less? Does multiculturalism have any chance whatsoever of converting the white suburbanites who glared at the television during the days of the riot, as all their stereotypes of the Dark Other were confirmed, or who bought handguns anticipating that the Dark Other would charge through the patio door?

These questions are perhaps unanswerable. We must begin by acknowledging the limits of multiculturalism. This is not a panacea. We will not find salvation. We must not exchange one religion for another. Neither can we afford to sanitize multiculturalism, satisfied with the Latin American market on Diversity Day at the local high school. (I actually gave a reading at a high school on "Diversity Day," and was interrupted at noon by the official loudspeaker announcement that "Diversity Day is now over!") There are always the perils of hand-holding sentimentality or sniffing condescension. Tokenism is tokenism, and beware expropriation.

And yet, the answer is more multiculturalism, not less. Hopefully, more multiculturalism will generate more respect among people, whether in the classroom or on television, in the bookstore or the movie theater, at the community center or a street festival. A truly critical multicultural approach to history is vital here: Children who learn the history of lynching in this country could point to the videotape of the Rodney King beating and say, "I read about this in school." The presence of multiculturalism in our lives as a real, tangible force would mean that Rodney King could no longer be regarded as a mere abstraction. He is a human being, so reminiscent of other African-American human beings we know and cherish, that his humiliation becomes their humiliation, and ours.

True, the movement for multiculturalism may be too late for the most desperate, those who must riot, who must speak what Martin Luther King called "the language of the unheard." Neither will multiculturalism reach those in love with their own racism. But a multicultural point of view may well reach the children of the rioters and the racists.

In times of crisis, the state and its corporate media will endeavor to divide us. A multicultural analysis will resist that urge to divide, that aggravation of genuine or invented tensions. During the riots in Los Angeles, African-Americans were portrayed as the aggressors. Nothing was said about African-American victims of the riots. Koreans protecting their businesses with guns were paraded by the media as evidence of African-American racism. Nothing was said about Asian rioters. A white truck driver was beaten by African-Americans, again on videotape, which served to portray whites solely as victims of violence. Nothing was said about white rioters, or the lethal retaliation of white police. Latinos were rendered invisible, despite the fact that nearly half the businesses destroyed and nearly half the people arrested were Latino. The media message: The races are hopelessly polarized. Lock your doors.

Thus divided from one another, people were less likely to notice reports of more than fifty dead in Los Angeles, many—no one knows how many—killed by the same police force whose brutality has been documented by Amnesty International. In this state of distraction, people were unlikely to notice the mass deportation of Latinos back to México and Central America following their arrest for anything from petty theft to a mere curfew violation. The citizenry might forget the name of Lawrence Powell, the police officer who led the beating of Rodney King, "the killer who kills today for five million killers who wish a killing," in the words of Carl Sandburg. Some of us were more likely to accept the bizarre explanation of the riots offered by the Bush administration, that the Great Society social programs of the 1960s were to blame. Multicultural solidarity—slowly taught, slowly learned—strikes at the heart of that imperial dictum: Divide and rule.

Ultimately, the advocates of multiculturalism must organize themselves. There must be national organizations, able to coordinate national action. There must be not one magazine or newsletter, but many. There must be more multicultural daycare centers and art centers and community centers. There must be more truly multicultural literary programs. There must be more multicultural anthologies, but we must write them; there must be more multicultural art exhibits, but we must create them; there must be more courses with a multicultural perspective, but we must teach them. The poet June Jordan said it: "We are the ones we have been waiting for."

Multiculturalism should not be simply a campus phenomenon. To confine multiculturalism to college campuses only would be to cultivate a monastery garden. Let multiculturalism be the language of adult education programs and prison writing workshops, barrio teen centers and inner-city preschools, wherever people gather to teach and be taught.

I return to a broad definition of multiculturalism: not only an approach, but a movement. As such, we can learn from the history of other movements, whether for civil rights or for women's suffrage or for the rights of labor: the strike, the boycott, the coalition, the raising of consciousness. As Fredrick Douglass advised: "Agitate, agitate."

III. POETRY LIKE BREAD

Poetry Like Bread

Poets of the Political Imagination

~ ~

In his landmark essay, "In Defense of the Word," Eduardo Galeano writes: "We are what we do, especially what we do to change what we are.... A literature born in the process of crisis and change, and deeply immersed in the risks and events of its time, can indeed help to create the symbols of the new reality, and perhaps—if talent and courage are not lacking—throw light on the signs along the road.... To claim that literature on its own is going to change reality would be an act of madness or arrogance. It seems to me no less foolish to deny that it can aid in making this change."

This essay will focus on the political imagination of certain contemporary American poets published by Curbstone Press of Willimantic, Connecticut. These poets are "American" not in the conventional sense of the United

States alone, but in the sense of "América" with an accent. Poets from New York, yes, but also Tegucigalpa. In this meeting of North and South we find a striking commonality of purpose and tactic, a solidarity born of the fact that one's own quiet labor in the dark is the shadow of the same act committed by others in the same clandestine dark thousands of miles away.

Poetry of the political imagination is a matter of both vision and language. Any progressive social change must be imagined first, and that vision must find its most eloquent possible expression to move from vision to reality. Any oppressive social condition, before it can change, must be named and condemned in words that persuade by stirring the emotions, awakening the senses. Thus the need for the political imagination.

Political imagination goes beyond protest to articulate an *artistry* of dissent. The question is not whether poetry and politics can mix. That question is a luxury for those who can afford it. The question is how *best* to combine poetry and politics, craft and commitment, how to find the artistic imagination equal to the intensity of the experience and the quality of the ideas.

There is a great poetic tradition of the political imagination in the Americas, embodied by Walt Whitman in the North and Pablo Neruda in the South. In his 1855 introduction to *Leaves of Grass*, Whitman indicates that the duty of the poet is "to cheer up slaves and horrify despots." In Neruda we encounter Whitman's most eloquent descendant. Radicalized by the Spanish Civil War, he articulates his metamorphosis in "I Explain a Few Things": "You will ask: why does your poetry / not speak to us of sleep, of the leaves, / of the great volcanoes of your native land? / Come and see the blood in the streets, / come and see / the blood in the streets, / come and see the blood / in the streets!"

The language produced by this political imagination is often clear, concrete, urgently direct. Though sometimes written to be read aloud, these are not campaign speeches. The appeal to the senses, the image, is still there: What better way to describe the haze in a polluted sky than Jack Hirschman's "tortillas of smog"? Indeed, poets of the political imagination often have the art of metaphor, of finding the face which is many faces, of finding the moment which stands for a century. Ernesto Cardenal's captured—and liberated—parrots become rebellious guerrillas in Nicaragua; Roque Dalton's torture victim looks up at the "perfect" glass eye of his torturer, made in the United States, and sees the physical manifestation of U.S. foreign policy in El Salvador.

~~

Though some political works are solely works of the imagination, many, if not most, are drawn directly from lived experience, contradicting a certain critical notion that political poems are written after a morning reading the newspaper, as the poet searches for a headline which will be sufficiently infuriating to inspire a burst of rhetoric. Many, if not most, political poets are personally familiar with the rhythms of oppression. The reader only has to encounter the startling prison poems of Jimmy Santiago Baca to appreciate that particular music. A social horror is focused through the prism of the poet's understanding, and the reader unfamiliar with the experience finds his or her own imagination engaged and politicized. Or the experience may prove surprisingly familiar: Virtually anyone who reads Baca's "I Applied for the Board," about the denial of parole, can identify with the trajectory of anticipation and disappointment sketched in the poem.

More than mere victims, however, poets of the political imagination are activists, political participants. Jack Hirschman and Sara Menefee fight for the rights of the homeless in San Francisco. Kevin Bowen is the head of an agency which serves Vietnam veterans and works towards a reconciliation with Vietnam. Luis Rodríguez works with peacemakers among gangs in Los Angeles and elsewhere. Victor Montejo, from exile, speaks out publicly against the suffering of his own Mayan people in Guatemala. In Latin America, a number of contemporary poets have engaged in the deeply political act of armed insurrection, including Roque Dalton, Otto René Castillo, Leonel Rugama, and Daisy Zamora.

Three of these four poets—Dalton, Castillo, and Rugama—were murdered for political reasons; most grotesquely of all, Castillo was burned alive by the Guatemalan military in 1967. Throughout the Americas, contemporary poets of the political imagination have been incarcerated, some for days, others for many years (including, of the poets mentioned above, Dalton, Castillo, Montejo, Hirschman, Menefee, and Rodríguez). Many more have been forced into political exile. Some have suffered unique forms of political persecution, as with the U.S. government's attempts to deport Margaret Randall.

Not surprisingly, resistance is a major theme of the political imagination. The poets are careful to insist upon the kind of intimate details that give politics a human face. Thus Jimmy Santiago Baca reports to us, from the midst of a prison rebellion, of men singing, "in the smoke and bars in their cells, they sing!" As a combatant in the Sandinista revolution, Daisy Zamora vividly recalls a friend making his way across a battlefield through "sporadic bursts of gunfire," as she and others watched, "our hearts beating uselessly." While some poets speak openly of political insurgency, others focus on the personal revolution of thought and language, which in turn become liberating forces. So Clemente Soto Vélez, another poet imprisoned for sedition, writes of "the thinking peon," the "peon of the subversive verb." As this vocabulary makes clear, the poets rightly regard their verbs as subversive, each poem as a political act in itself.

The same poets are committed advocates, speaking for the voices struck silent, living or dead. The poets tell us of being haunted by this song of the voiceless. In "Nocturnal Visits," Claribel Alegría speaks of "the amputated / the cripples / those who lost both legs / both eyes / the stammering teenagers. / At night I listen to their phantoms / shouting in my ear." In "Then Comes a Day," Luis Rodríguez visits a barrio cemetery filled with his dead friends and writes: "I have carried the obligation to these names. / I have honored their voices / still reverberating through me." Gioconda Belli remembers Nicaragua's dead in "The Blood of Others" and "In Memoriam." Indeed, these are poets who pay tribute to their dead, so many dead, from the internationally known, such as Víctor Jara, the singer and guitarist slain by the military in the Chilean coup, to the anonymous, who would dissolve into oblivion without the poets.

Both Whitman and Neruda expressly embraced the role of the poet as advocate, and in so doing influenced generations of poets. Whitman, in #24 of "Song of Myself," proclaims: "through me many long dumb voices, / voices of the interminable generations of prisoners and slaves, / voices of the diseas'd and despairing and of thieves and dwarfs ... voices veiled and I remove the veil." Neruda, standing at *The*

Heights of Macchu Picchu, speaking to centuries of dead laborers, says in Canto 12: "Look at me from the depths of the earth, / tiller of fields, weaver, reticent shepherd ... jeweler with crushed fingers, / farmer anxious among his seedlings, / potter wasted among his clays ... I come to speak for your dead mouths." The poet's advocacy springs from compassion, and compassion is the poet's pulse. Whitman again: "whoever walks a furlong without sympathy walks to / his own funeral drest in his shroud."

The poems of the political imagination document daily existence as well, finding the political in the everyday. There is, for example, invaluable documentation of working-class lives and the struggle to transcend dehumanizing labor. Leo Connellan movingly writes of Amelia, a woman of the canneries in Maine. Kevin Bowen brings us the "Gelatin Factory," and Luis Rodríguez "The Blast Furnace." Cheryl Savageau tells of dangerous work with silicon, pesticides, and asbestos. There is unemployment too, as in Savageau's "Department of Labor Haiku": "In the winter snow / the kitchens fill up with steam / and men out of work."

They also document the presence of such social forces as racism and sexism, and in so doing make those abstract terms painfully concrete. Tino Villanueva constructs the personification of anti-Mexican bigotry in his portrayal of Sarge, a character from the movie *Giant* who enforces, with his "thick arms," the rules of segregation in a Texas diner. The major Puerto Rican poet Julia de Burgos, before her early death, anticipated the rise of feminism with "To Julia de Burgos," a condemnation of suffocating social convention: "who governs in me is me."

These poems not only condemn, but appreciate. Claribel Alegría appreciates Carmen Bomba, "porter ... human beast of burden" and "poet." Jimmy Santiago Baca, as one who has known brutal incarceration, can proclaim, "Ah Rain!" and mean it, passionately, politically. Jack Hirschman pauses at a political rally to observe a butterfly walking across a newspaper in "This Neruda Earth."

In fact, perhaps the most remarkable characteristic found in the poetry of the political imagination is the quality of hopefulness, testimony to the extraordinary resilience of that human quality. The prophetic voice resonates throughout the poetry; the poets sing of the possibility, the *certainty* of eventual justice. Alegría, a poet "condemned so many times / to be a crow," is able to fly, "and amid valleys / volcanos / and debris of war / I catch sight of the promised land." Soto Vélez, also a poet of the "promised land," predicts that "the hands / of the peon" will "thunder in the cartilage of the future." Alfonso Quijada Urías of El Salvador envisions a time when the grocer will use the poet's writings as paper funnels "to wrap up his sugar and coffee / for the people of the future / who now for obvious reasons / cannot savor his sugar nor his coffee." Most poignantly, the murdered Castillo writes that it is "splendid / to know yourself victorious / when all around you / it's all still so cold, / so dark."

This is the height of political imagination, in the sense of the poet as visionary, again echoing Neruda and Whitman. Neruda could peer back into history and foresee contemporary resistance movements in México and Perú with his poems for Emilano Zapata and Tupac Amarú—movements, in fact, which would adopt the very names of these revolutionaries. Whitman could gaze upon the slave at auction and see "the father of those who shall be fathers in their turns, / In him the start of populous states and rich republics, / Of him countless immortal lives with countless embodiments and enjoyments."

What else but defiant, extravagant hope—political imagination—could motivate Roque Dalton, a man who suffered imprisonment and ultimately assassination, to write: "I believe the world is beautiful / and that poetry, like bread, is for everyone."

The Good Liar
Meets His Executioners

The Evolution of a Poem

~ ~

Don't lie. This admonition booms in our ears from early childhood. A liar, a teller of lies, is to be shunned, evicted from job or home, sometimes even imprisoned. Yet, the most astonishing liar I ever met was an honest man, truthful even about the fact that he wore no pants on the day he faced the firing squad.

Nelson Azócar is a friend of mine. We worked together as tenant lawyers for Su Clínica Legal, the legal services program for the Latino community in Chelsea, Massachusetts. Nelson came from Chile, a man who would sometimes erupt in song when he saw me—"¡Martín, que toca violín!"—but whose face was rounded with quiet dignity, a gravity which suggested that he knew the burden of an extraordinary and devastating experience.

On September 11, 1973, a savage military coup overthrew the elected government of President Salvador Allende in Chile. A military junta assumed power, headed by General Augusto Pinochet. This was pure state terror: executions, imprisonment, and disappearances for all those stained red by leftist ideas. Over the years, in snatches of conversation, I heard Nelson tell the story of his escape from Chile. I learned that I had been working with a man who once talked his way out of being shot by a firing squad. I asked him how anyone could be so persuasive under such terrific pressure. "You have to be a good liar," he grinned.

I began to compose a poem in 1991. The first draft of the poem told Nelson's story in simple linear fashion. Actually, Nelson had not one, but three encounters with military authority. The first incident involved interrogation by a military tribunal. The second occurred when Nelson tried to leave the country and a suspicious officer confronted him with a gun. The third took place when soldiers removed him from his mother's house for an appointment with the firing squad. Each time, the good liar outwitted his executioners.

In fact, I called the poem, "The Good Liar Meets His Executioners," in honor of Nelson's uncommon gift. The poem ended: "he tells what he knows three times / what the lie is / who the liars." The word "liar," of course, was used subversively, to tunnel through the usual associations. If Nelson told justifiable, "good" lies—to save his own life in a dangerous situation—then Pinochet and Chile's junta told enormous lies, which justified a cascade of murder and repression in the name of fighting communism.

Yet, I was not satisfied with the poem. This was bland stew, missing some mysterious spice. I revised the poem many times, to no avail. When I published a book in 1993, I omitted this poem. I put Nelson's tale in my desk and forgot it.

The following year, I began reviewing Pablo Neruda in preparation for teaching a course on his poetry. Neruda died twelve days after the military takeover; his funeral was the first public demonstration in Chile against the coup. I took out Nelson's poem. Since Nelson's experience was, in effect, a metaphor for liberation through intelligence and determination, the poem needed a metaphor for liberation to recur in every stanza. Moreover, Nelson's escape was a secular miracle. The poem needed that sense of the miraculous, the fantastic, reminiscent of certain Neruda poems.

The sea, Neruda's muse at Isla Negra, provided the metaphor for liberation. The sea also lends itself to images of the miraculous. In the second stanza, when Nelson devised "a plan to leave Chile by sea," I added: "Somewhere the waves / rumbled a prayer for him / like a chorus of monks." After the escape plan failed, in the fourth stanza, now came this: "Somewhere the sea turtles / lumbered from the surf / and waited all night for him." After he talked his way out of being executed, at the end of the sixth stanza, these lines now occurred: "Somewhere the ocean boiled for him, / as if here a giant octopus had wrapped itself / around a warship full of admirals." Finally, characterizing his escape, in the last stanza, I added that Nelson "smuggled himself away from Chile / the green waves lifting him."

Then came another new motif: I repeated the phrases "good liar" and "executioners" in each of the first six stanzas, but only repeated the phrase "good liar" in the seventh and final stanza. The idea was to convey the churning cyle of oppression and resistance. If oppression returns again and again, so too does resistance, in a constant loop of human history. Here, resistance—"the good liar"—is even more resilient than oppression—"the executioners"—and so has the last word in the poem.

There remained one more step: reading the poem to Nelson. I gave a reading at the Chelsea public library, where I showed him the poem, gave him a copy, then asked his permission to read it aloud. I told the audience that I was grateful to him, because the subject of the poem is, in a way, the co-author of the poem.

That night, I received a call from Nelson. He politely asked if he was really the co-author, as I said that afternoon. Of course, I responded. Nelson then told me that I should make two changes. "First," he said, "you have sea turtles in the poem. In Chile, on the Pacific Coast, we have sea lions. They should be sea lions. Second," he went on, "when the soldiers take me away to shoot me, you have me dressed in my bathrobe. I know you're trying to protect my dignity, but the truth is that they took me away in my underwear. It's important to say that."

He was right. I made the changes, and included the poem in my next book, published in 1996. The poem took five years to finish, an act of endurance, surely, but nothing compared to the endurance of Nelson Azócar in the escape from his executioners.

The Good Liar
Meets His Executioners

for Nelson Azócar, Valparaíso, Chile

The first time
the good liar
met his executioners

was at the military tribunal
after the coup.
Before the row of officers,
withered stiff as scarecrows,
he grew more polite and forgetful
with each name tolled
on the list: *"No, señor. No, señor."*
On the wall, the portrait of General Pinochet,
mustache and sunglasses, glowering.

The good liar returned home that day,
but singers of red songs
reddened the waters of Chile
face down in the current,
and the executioners kept vigil
over blazing pyramids of books,
so a passport was forged
with a plan to leave Chile by sea.
Somewhere the waves
rumbled a prayer for him
like a chorus of monks.

The second time
the good liar
met his executioners
was at the dock,
hunched in a peacoat
with a sack on his shoulder.
A pistol dug into his neck,
chamber clicked
like a bored sargeant
cracking his knuckles.
A guard disbelieved the passport

stamped Merchant Marine,
the list of names quivering
in his other hand.

"My name is not on that list,"
the good liar said,
and since his executioner
could not read
without trailing a finger slowly
across the page,
the pistol relaxed, leaving
the imprint of the barrel,
and only the passport was burned.
Somewhere the sea lions
lumbered from the surf
and waited all night for him.

The third time
the good liar
met his executioners
was at the house of his mother.
Now his name was on the list,
troops rifle-jabbing him
still in his underwear
to the pickup truck,
family on the sidewalk
begging to give him
at least the dignity of his pants,
neighbors listening with bowed heads.

On the way to the firing squad,
a balding hill where every skull
recalled the bullet's cloud of ink

flooding the brain,
the good liar invented fables
of a colonel he knew,
barbeques in the backyard
and dating his daughter,
boasting to the other
condemned compañeros
loud enough
for curious executioners to believe.
The truck circled back
and left him at the jail instead,
thirty men in a room
jostling for a peephole to breathe
or a rubber pot rocking with piss.
Somewhere the ocean boiled for him,
as if here a giant octopus had wrapped itself
around a warship full of admirals.

After bail, the good liar
smuggled himself away from Chile,
the green waves lifting him.
You have to be a good liar, he says.
In the sanctuary of steaming coffee
he tells what he knows three times,
what the lie is,
who the liars.

The Poetics of Commerce

The Nike Poetry Slam

~~

I confess that I am a poet of situations. I have written poems for weddings, birthdays, and holidays. I wrote a New Year's poem for the radio. I wrote a poem for the 25th anniversary of a magazine, and so the number 25 had to be featured in the poem. I even wrote a poem called "Pitching the Potatoes" for an anthology of poems about potatoes. Then I was asked to write a poem for a Nike commercial. This was the Nike Poetry Slam.

It *is* possible to write a good shoe poem. Here is my favorite poem about shoes, written by Jack Agüeros:

Psalm for Distribution

Lord,
On 8th Street
Between 6th Avenue and Broadway
In Greenwich Village
There are enough shoe stores
With enough shoes
To make me wonder
Why there are shoeless people
On the earth.
Lord,
You have to fire the Angel
In charge of distribution.

This is probably not the kind of shoe poem contemplated by the creators of the Nike Poetry Slam.

Global Exchange, a human rights organization in San Francisco, has developed a "Nike Chronology" based on documentation of company labor practices in Asia. In March 1996, fifteen women were hit on the head and neck with a Nike sneaker for "poor" work at the Sam Yang factory in Vietnam. In November 1996, CBS aired a *48 Hours* documentary on similar abuses in Vietnam. Nike workers were forced to kneel with their hands in the air for twenty-five minutes as punishment, another worker had her mouth taped shut for talking, and two more workers reported an attempted rape by a Nike factory supervisor at the Tae Kwang Vina factory. On March 8, 1997, International Women's Day, fifty-six women were forced to run outside the Nike factory in the Dong Nai province because they did not wear regulation shoes. A dozen women collapsed due to heat exhaustion and spent the day in the hospital. This incident was reported by Bob Herbert in *The New York Times*.

Then there are wages. Children in Pakistan stitch Nike soccer balls for 60 cents a day, according to Sydney Schanberg in *Life* magazine. Bob Herbert reported a study by Thuyen Nguyen, a Vietnamese-American businessman, which revealed that Nike workers in Vietnam earn $1.60 a day, while the average cost of three meals a day is $2.10. Global Exchange has also chronicled Nike's crackdown on the strikes in their factories, a predictable consequence of the struggle over wages. In January 1993, twenty-four workers accused of organizing a strike at the Sung Hwa Dunia factory in Indonesia were fired. Likewise, workers in the Assembly Production Department at the Wellco Factory in China struck for their full wages in March 1997 and were all dismissed.

The common response to reports that U.S. companies are operating Third World sweatshops is an acknowledgment that conditions are spartan, followed closely by the assertion that these jobs are nonetheless superior to anything found elsewhere in that particular country. *The Christian Science Monitor* relayed these comments by Michael Hooker, Chancellor of the University of North Carolina-Chapel Hill, defending the university's multimillion dollar contract with Nike: "The working conditions, relative to what else is available to them, are really very good. So people are clamoring for those jobs." Nike spokesman Vada Manager told *The New York Times* that "Nike workers earn superior wages and manufacture the product under superior conditions."

Yet, Global Exchange maintains that Nike did not pay the local minimum wage ($2.46 a day in Jakarta) to Indonesian workers until April 1997. *Business Week* reported on an internal audit at Nike which showed that the company paid its workers in Vietnam 20 percent less than the minimum wage of 19 cents per hour. This may explain why the workers at Sarn Yang Vina factory struck in April 1997 for a raise of one penny an hour. As for "superior conditions," Nat Hentoff in *The Village Voice* cited that same internal audit, which "tells of a factory near Ho Chi Minh City where the level of carcinogens exceeded Vietnamese standards by six to 177 times in parts of the plant.... 77 percent of the workers are already afflicted with respiratory problems."

Meanwhile, according to *The New York Times,* Nike reported sales of $9.2 billion in 1996. Bob Herbert summed up the significance of Nike with bitter eloquence: "Nike is important because it epitomizes the triumph of monetary values over all others, and the corresponding devaluation of those peculiar interests and values we once thought of as human." Nike's response to all the controversy, in Herbert's words, is "an elaborate international public relations campaign to give the appearance that it cares about the workers." This goes hand-in-hand with "advertising campaigns that are so slick, so hip, and so compelling that consumers feel that, whatever the price, they must wear the product." Thus the Nike Poetry Slam.

A poetry slam is, of course, a staged competition among poets, part of the "performance poetry" or "spoken word" phenomenon which has developed an enthusiastic following in the youth market so treasured by Nike. The Nike Poetry Slam required that poets compete by writing verse for commercials in praise of certain female athletes—Nike athletes participating in the 1998 Winter Olympics.

This was part of Nike's larger ad campaign built around the female athlete, which a coalition of women's groups has identified as wildly ironic, given Nike's treatment of female workers in Asia.

As articulated by Matthew Rothschild in the January 1998 issue of *The Progressive* magazine, "Nike, one of the kings of cooptation ... ever vigilant on the cultural front, wants to capitalize" on the poetry slams. So who are "Nike's Poets"? Rothschild advised: "Watch for those Nike ads that run during the 1998 Winter Olympics so you can pick out the poets who change the oil for the industry of hip consumerism."

What follows is the correspondence between Nike's ad agency and me. (And yes, they spelled "Massachusetts" wrong.)

•   ~~~

Goodby, Silverstein & Partners
October 14, 1997

Mr. Martin Espada
University of Massachusettes at Amherst
Bartlett Hall Rm. 251
Amherst, Massachusettes 01003

Re: Nike Poetry Slam

Dear Mr. Espada:

The enclosed package contains what we hope will be an unusual and interesting project for you.

We are developing a series of four commercials, which will be aired on national television during the 1998 Winter Olympics. Each commercial will feature an outstanding and inspiring female athlete, sponsored by our client, Nike.

We hope these short films will celebrate the poetry of competition and athletics by using your words.

Detail follows in the proposal. All poems need to be submitted, using shipping materials to be provided, by November 1, 1997.

We are anxious to know about your participation and would like to confirm your involvement by October 22. If you have questions, please feel free to call me […]. As well, we would like to confirm your involvement and address for delivery of video and shipping materials by October 22 with a call to the same number.

In advance, we thank you for your time to review and respond.

Sincerely,

Cindy Fluitt
Producer

~~~

A Proposal to a Few Select Poets for the Nike Poetry Slam

This year's Winter Olympic Games in Nagano, Japan will be unlike any before. Women will compete in greater numbers, in more sports. And for perhaps the first time, a large number of female competitors will be athletes who grew up feeling empowered, supported and equal to their male counterparts when it came to athletic opportunities, facilities and training.

It is a rare, historic change and with your help, we want to applaud it.

We would like to celebrate four of the most remarkable of the new women athletes in a series of commercial films that will run during the Olympic telecasts. And we'd like to do it through the eyes of artists like yourselves. You each have a voice, outlook and perspective on the world that we feel mirrors, in some fashion, the spirit these athletes possess.

Read the accompanying biographies of Picabo Street, Dawn Staley, Cammi Granato and Mia Hamm. Watch the videotapes. If you don't know these athletes now, we feel sure you'll soon find them unique: uniquely committed to the rigors of sport at the highest levels, uniquely aware of their roles in history.

Then write about one of them. Or each of them. Or all of them at once. It could be about their roles in the world of sports, their individual styles, the significance of their contributions.

Ultimately, of course, you are free to write anything you want. We will not censor your thoughts or opinions or feelings. You don't have to write about shoes or even mention Nike. This is not meant to be a commercial: It is meant to be a showcase for these athletes and for your work. (For legal reasons, you should not include references to the Olympics, Games or medals. And keep in mind TV network standards and practices regarding content and language.)

It must be possible for your poem to be read out loud in less than 30 seconds. (Otherwise, we may have to edit your piece for time.) Unfortunately, the mechanics of commerce outweigh the demands of art in this instance.

You may submit your work to us in writing, or even better, videotape yourself reading the piece.

We will be illustrating the poems in short films that will work rather like rock videos. Perhaps you will be in the film, perhaps not. Creative input will be welcome, but remains the responsibility of the creative team and client.

All poems submitted become the property of Nike, with rights to display, edit for length and publish. There is a $250 fee paid for one or more submissions by November 1 and a $2500 prize if we choose your work for the project. If you would prefer, we will donate this prize to a charity of your choice.

We are also approaching a few select high schools for poetry submissions from their students.

Videotapes, releases and shipping information will be forthcoming when we determine your interest and availability.

Thank you and good luck. We look forward to hearing your work.

October 22, 1997

Cindy Fluitt, Producer
Goodby, Silverstein & Partners
720 California Street
San Francisco, CA 94108

Re: Nike Poetry Slam

Dear Ms. Fluitt:

This is a letter in response to your correspondence concerning the
Nike Poetry Slam and my proposed participation.

I could reject your offer based on the fact that your deadline is
ludicrous (i.e. ten days from the above date). A poem is not a
pop tart.

I could reject your offer based on the fact that I would not be free
to write whatever I want, notwithstanding your assurances to the
contrary, since I must "keep in mind TV network standards and
practices regarding content and language." You clearly have no
idea what the word "censorship" means. Where, as you put it, "the
mechanics of commerce outweigh the demands of art," then de
facto censorship will flourish.

I could reject your offer based on the fact that, to make this offer to
me in the first place, you must be totally and insultingly ignorant
of my work as a poet, which strives to stand against all that you
and your client represent. Whoever referred me to you did you a
grave disservice.

I could reject your offer based on the fact that your client, Nike,
has through commercials such as these outrageously manipulated
the youth market, so that even low-income adolescents are
compelled to buy products they do not need at prices they cannot
afford.

Ultimately, however, I am rejecting your offer as a protest against
the brutal labor practices of Nike. I will not associate myself with a
company that engages in the well-documented exploitation of

workers in sweatshops. Please spare me the usual corporate response: there's no problem, and besides, we're working on it. I suggest, instead, that you take the $2500 you now dangle before me and distribute that money equally among the laborers in an Asian sweatshop doing business with Nike. The funds would be much more useful to them than to me. Thank you.

Sincerely,

Martín Espada

All Things Censored

The Poem NPR
Doesn't Want You to Hear

~~~

I was an NPR poet. In particular, I was an *All Things Considered* poet. *All Things Considered* would occasionally broadcast my poems in conjunction with news stories. One producer even commissioned a New Year's poem from me. "Imagine the Angels of Bread" aired on January 2, 1994, in the same broadcast as the news of the Zapatista uprising in Chiapas. But now I have been censored by *All Things Considered* and National Public Radio because I wrote a poem for them about Mumia Abu-Jamal.

As many readers may know, Mumia Abu-Jamal is an eloquent African-American journalist on death row, convicted in the 1981 slaying of police officer Daniel Faulkner in Philadelphia—under extremely dubious circumstances.

Officer Faulkner was beating Mumia's brother with a flashlight when Mumia came upon the scene. In the ensuing confrontation, both Faulkner and Mumia were shot. Though Mumia had a .38 caliber pistol in his taxi that night, and the gun was found at the scene, the judgment of the medical examiner concerning the fatal bullet was that it came from a .44 caliber weapon. Several witnesses reported seeing an unidentified gunman flee, leaving Faulkner and Mumia severely wounded in the street.

What happened in court was a tragic pantomime. The trial featured a prosecutor who assailed Mumia for his radical politics, including his teenaged membership in the Black Panthers. Witnesses were coached and coerced in their testimony or intimidated into silence by police. The trial was presided over by a judge notorious for handing out death sentences to Black defendants, or manipulating juries to do the same, as in this case. A strong critic of the Philadelphia police—particularly with respect to their brutal treatment of the African-American collective called MOVE—Mumia was condemned by the very system he questioned.

In August 1995, Mumia came within ten days of being executed by lethal injection. He is seeking a new trial. Robert Meeropol, the younger son of Julius and Ethel Rosenberg, says: "Mumia is the first political prisoner in the U.S. to face execution since my parents."

Enter NPR. In 1994, National Public Radio agreed to broadcast a series of Mumia's radio commentaries from death row. The Prison Radio Project produced the recordings that April. Suddenly, NPR canceled the commentaries under pressure from the right, particularly the Fraternal Order of Police and Senator Robert Dole. Mumia and the Prison Radio Project sued NPR on First Amendment grounds.

In April 1997, I was contacted by the staff at *All Things Considered*, their first communication since my New Year's poem. Diantha Parker and Sara Sarasohn commissioned me to write a poem for National Poetry Month. The general idea was that the poem should be like a news story, with a journalistic perspective. They suggested that I write a poem in response to a news story in a city I visited during the month. Ms. Parker called to obtain my itinerary, so that NPR could give me an assignment relevant to a particular city. Fatefully, they could think of no such assignment. But the idea had found a home in the folds of my brain.

Since April is National Poetry Month, I traveled everywhere. I went from Joplin, Missouri, to Kansas City, to Rochester, to Chicago, to Camden, New Jersey. And then to Philadelphia. I read an article in the April 16th *Philadelphia Weekly* about Mumia Abu-Jamal. The article described a motion by one of Mumia's lawyers, Leonard Weinglass, to introduce testimony by an unnamed prostitute with new information about the case. This became the catalyst for the poem.

I also visited the tomb of Walt Whitman in nearby Camden, and was moved. Whitman wrote this in "Song of Myself": "The runaway slave came to my house and stopt outside, / I heard his motions crackling the twigs of the wood pile, / Through the swung half-door of the kitchen I saw him limpsy and weak, / And went where he sat on a log and led him in and assured him, / And brought water and fill'd a tub for his sweated body and bruis'd feet." In my poem, Whitman's tomb became a place of refuge for the "fugitive slave," first for a nameless prostitute, then Mumia. By poem's end, this place and poet came to represent our sacred compassion, our ceremonies of conscience, our will to resist, our refusal to forget.

I faxed the poem to NPR on April 21st. On April 24th, *All Things Considered* staff informed me that they would not air the poem. They were explicit: They would not air the poem because of its subject matter—Mumia Abu-Jamal—and its political sympathies.

"NPR is refusing to air this poem because of its political content?" I asked. "Yes," said Diantha Parker.

She cited the "history" of NPR and Mumia, a reference to their refusal to air his commentaries. She further explained that the poem was "not the way NPR wants to return to this subject." Such is the elegant bureaucratic language of censorship. Parker would later admit, in an interview with Dennis Bernstein of KPFA-FM, that she "loved" the poem, and that "the poem should have run, perhaps in a different context." This comment also debunks the idea that NPR was merely exercising its editorial discretion. The quality of the poem was never questioned. The criteria for the assignment had been met. "He did everything we asked him to do," said Parker to Bernstein.

A few days later, I met Marilyn Jamal, Mumia's former wife. I presented her with the poem and watched her struggle against tears. Then she said: "I promised myself that I wouldn't cry anymore." I concluded that NPR's censorship should come to light.

The people at *All Things Considered* had expressed indignation that I was aware of their "history" with Mumia, and still wrote the poem anyway. Sara Sarasohn, the same producer who solicited my New Year's poem, told me: "We never expected you would write *this!*" Said Parker to Dennis Bernstein: "He should have known better."

How could I not write this poem once it came to me? How could I censor my imagination, making myself complicit in NPR's muzzling of Mumia?

I had given NPR the proverbial benefit of the doubt. I had hoped that a sense of fairness—a respect for opposing viewpoints—would compel *All Things Considered* to broadcast the poem, a broadcast which would address the concerns of listeners who felt that NPR "sold out" Mumia. Instead, I encountered a reaction based on cowardice and self-pity.

Confronted with the fate of a man on death row, the staff of *All Things Considered* could only think of their own discomfort, their own problems caused by the controversy, their own political and professional security. Worse, they insisted on implicitly comparing their suffering to the suffering of Mumia Abu-Jamal. Diantha Parker cited "safety concerns" for NPR staff in explaining the refusal to air a poem about a man facing execution. When contacted by Demetria Martínez, a columnist for the *National Catholic Reporter*, concerning this story, executive producer Ellen Weiss complained that the NPR-Mumia controversy "will follow me to my tombstone." *Her tombstone.* Compare this to the tombstone of a man who may soon die by lethal injection. Surely, Weiss deserves the Liberal Media Sensitivity to Language Award.

Weiss, who at the time of this interview had not read the poem, also informed Martínez that NPR had a policy of not airing any commentaries or "op-ed" pieces about Mumia Abu-Jamal while his lawsuit against NPR was pending. Note how a poem became a "commentary," not a work of art, when that definition justified censorship. Strangely, the two people who made the decision not to air the poem, and informed me of that decision—Parker and Sarasohn—never mentioned such a policy in a telephone conversation of almost twenty minutes. Yet, some weeks later, Sarasohn told Dennis Bernstein: "It's a legal thing." Parker and Sarasohn also confessed to Bernstein that they did not consult their supervisors or NPR attorneys before deciding to suppress the poem.

The legal justification for this act of censorship amused me; apparently, the people at NPR forgot that I am also a lawyer. As fellow attorney Bill Newman, head of the western Massachusetts ACLU, pointed out, "The reason for silence in the face of pending litigation does not apply. As a poet, an independent person, you are not a corporate spokesman. You cannot bind the corporation. The reason corporations like NPR say 'no comment' is because they don't want the statements to be used against them in court. That rationale does not apply to a poet reading a poem. It makes no sense."

Furthermore, the subject of the lawsuit and the subject of the poem were totally different. The censored poem was not about Mumia's censored commentaries, nor about his First Amendment rights. Mumia's lawsuit against NPR did not concern his criminal case or his possible execution. Newman raised a question: "If Mumia were to dismiss his lawsuit, would they air this poem?" (In fact, a federal district court judge dismissed the suit in September 1997. That decision has been appealed.) Dennis Bernstein asked both Sarasohn and Parker if the poem might be aired following Mumia's execution, as an elegy. Both times, his question was greeted by silence.

NPR's policy, even if ex post facto, served as a punitive means to perpetuate Mumia's silence by silencing those who would speak for him. "First they censor him. Then, because he exercises his First Amendment right to remedy the violation, NPR compounds that affront to his freedom of expression by refusing to allow others to comment on his behalf," said Newman.

Subsequent to the original publication of this article in the July 1997 issue of *The Progressive* magazine, NPR stopped using the legal argument publicly to justify its actions. Producers Parker and Sarasohn were no longer available for comment. Instead, Kathy Scott, Director of Communications for NPR, told *The Hartford Courant* that "We are a news organization and we don't take advocacy positions." Now the problem, apparently, was that "Espada was attempting to use NPR as an advocate for Mumia Abu-Jamal," as Scott expressed it in a statement to WCVB-TV in Boston. At one point, Scott said of Mumia: "My gosh, the man's life is at stake, and to influence that decision one way or another just would not be responsible on our part."

Like a top left spinning too long, NPR's spin had become wobbly. Newspapers and radio and television stations take positions, called "editorials," sometimes with the disclaimer that the opinions expressed in the editorial do not necessarily reflect those of management, a concept seemingly alien to the producers of *All Things Considered.*

In fact, NPR takes "advocacy positions" all the time. They are called "commentaries." Moreover, *All Things Considered* had aired my poems in the past—all poems of advocacy. The ultimate contradiction, however, was this: In July 1997, after discussions with NPR in Washington, WFCR-FM, the NPR affiliate in Amherst, Massachusetts, elected to air the poem in the context of a news story about the controversy. The poem was not used against NPR in court, nor was NPR's status as a news organization demolished by the presence on the air of an advocate for Mumia Abu-Jamal.

~~~~

I once asked my friend David Velasquez, who worked as a farrier, about shoeing horses. He replied: "Imagine a creature that weighs 1,500 pounds and is motivated by fear." That's NPR, at least in terms of Mumia. Of course, the liberal media is notorious for timidity. To again quote my wise friend: "A liberal is someone who leaves the room when a fight breaks out."

Editorial decisions are made for political reasons on a daily basis: Rarely, however, is the curtain lifted to reveal the corroded machinery. Moreover, as a left-wing poet, I expect to be censored by mainstream media. But when so-called "alternative" media also censor the left, the impact is devastating. Ask Mumia Abu-Jamal.

This censorship also manifests itself on the streets. In November 1997, I gave a benefit reading with a group of poets for the Western Pennsylvania Committee to Free Mumia Abu-Jamal. A member of the organization, a graduate student from Germany named Gabriele Gottlieb, was posting flyers for the event when she was attacked and seriously beaten by a man denouncing Mumia as a "cop-killer." Members of the Committee speculated that the attacker may have been an off-duty police officer. In less charitable moments, I imagine that he was essentially expressing the same urges as the people at *All Things Considered*, albeit more brutally.

Readers can call or write *All Things Considered* to urge that the poem be aired. They can urge, again, that Mumia's commentaries be aired, or at least released from the vaults of NPR so that others might have access to them. They can inform NPR that their financial contributions to National Public Radio will instead be diverted to the legal defense of Mumia Abu-Jamal. That address is: Committee to Save Mumia Abu-Jamal, 163 Amsterdam Avenue, #115, New York, NY 10023. Checks should be made payable to the Bill of Rights Foundation ("for MAJ").

Meanwhile, I assume that *All Things Considered* has put my name on their blacklist. I wonder what poems I must write to be allowed on *All Things Considered* again. Maybe some cowboy poetry.

What follows is the poem NPR does not want you to hear. I have made a few minor revisions, since, in the midst of this madness, with a poet's compulsive nature, I was trying to create a better poem.

Another Nameless Prostitute Says the Man is Innocent

for Mumia Abu-Jamal
Philadelphia, Pennsylvania/Camden, New Jersey,
April 1997

The board-blinded windows knew what happened;
the pavement sleepers of Philadelphia, groaning
in their ghost-infested sleep, knew what happened;
every Black man blessed
with the gashed eyebrow of nightsticks
knew what happened;
even Walt Whitman knew what happened,
poet a century dead, keeping vigil
from the tomb on the other side of the bridge.

More than fifteen years ago,
the cataract stare of the cruiser's headlights,
the impossible angle of the bullet,
the tributaries and lakes of blood,
Officer Faulkner dead, suspect Mumia shot in the chest,
the witnesses who saw a gunman
running away, his heart and feet thudding.

The nameless prostitutes know,
hunched at the curb, their bare legs chilled.
Their faces squinted to see that night,
rouged with fading bruises. Now the faces fade.
Perhaps an eyewitness putrifies eyes open in a bed of soil,
or floats in the warm gulf stream of her addiction,
or hides from the fanged whispers of the police
in the tomb of Walt Whitman,
where the granite door is open
and fugitive slaves may rest.

Mumia: the Panther beret, the thinking dreadlocks,
dissident words that swarmed the microphone like a hive,
sharing meals with people named Africa,
calling out their names even after the police bombardment
that charred their black bodies.
So the governor has signed the death warrant.
The executioner's needle would flush the poison
down into Mumia's writing hand
so the fingers curl like a burned spider;
his calm questioning mouth would grow numb,
and everywhere radios sputter to silence, in his memory.

The veiled prostitutes are gone,
gone to the segregated balcony of whores.

But the newspaper reports that another nameless prostitute
says the man is innocent, that she will testify at the next hearing.
Beyond the courthouse, a multitude of witnesses chants, prays,
shouts for his prison to collapse, a shack in a hurricane.

Mumia, if the last nameless prostitute
becomes an unraveling turban of steam,
if the judges' robes become clouds of ink
swirling like octopus deception,
if the shroud becomes your Amish quilt,
if your dreadlocks are snipped during autopsy,
then drift above the ruined RCA factory
that once birthed radios
to the tomb of Walt Whitman,
where the granite door is open
and fugitive slaves may rest.

Acknowledgments

These essays and poems first appeared or are forthcoming in different forms in the following publications, to whose editors grateful acknowledgment is made:

Facing the Lion (Beacon Press): "Zapata's Disciple and Perfect Brie"

Race Traitor: "Postcard from the Empire of Queen Ixolib"

Las Christmas (Knopf): "Argue Not Concerning God"

Muy Macho: Latino Men Confront Their Manhood (Anchor Books): "The Puerto Rican Dummy and the Merciful Son"

Tampa Review: "The Governor of Puerto Rico Reveals at His Inaugural That He is the Reincarnation of Ponce de León"

Luna: "The Janitor's Garden"

Diálogo: "The New Bathroom Policy at English High School: Dispatches from the Language Wars"

Art on the Line (Curbstone Press): "Multiculturalism in the Year of Columbus and Rodney King"

Poetry Like Bread (Curbstone Press): "Poetry Like Bread: Poets of the Political Imagination"

Literary Cavalcade: "The Good Liar Meets His Executioners: The Evolution of a Poem"

LIP: "The Poetics of Commerce: The Nike Poetry Slam"

The Progressive: "All Things Censored: The Poem NPR Doesn't Want You to Hear" and "Another Nameless Prostitute Says the Man is Innocent"

These poems are reprinted from the following collections of poetry by Martín Espada:

Trumpets from the Islands of Their Eviction (Bilingual Press): "Mariano Explains Yanqui Colonialism to Judge Collings"

Rebellion is the Circle of a Lover's Hands (Curbstone Press): "The New Bathroom Policy at English High School"

City of Coughing and Dead Radiators (W.W. Norton): "White Birch"

Imagine the Angels of Bread (W.W. Norton): "When the Leather is a Whip," "Because Clemente Means Merciful," "My Native Costume," "Governor Wilson of California Talks in His Sleep," "Offerings to an Ulcerated God," and "The Good Liar Meets His Executioners"

"Psalm for Distribution" by Jack Agüeros was originally published in *Correspondence Between the Stonehaulers* (New York: Hanging Loose Press, 1991). Reprinted by permission of the author.

Many thanks to Frank Espada, Katherine Gilbert-Espada, Global Exchange, Frances Goldin, Ray González, Lynn Lu, Matthew Rothschild, Esmeralda Santiago, Alexander Taylor, and the Vermont Studio Center for their support of this work.

Index

About the Author

Martin Espada was born in Brooklyn, New York, in 1957. He has published five books of poetry, most recently *City of Coughing and Dead Radiators* (W.W. Norton, 1993) and *Imagine the Angels of Bread* (W.W. Norton, 1996), which won an American Book Award and was a finalist for the National Book Critics' Circle Award. Another volume, *Rebellion is the Circle of a Lover's Hands* (Curbstone, 1990), won both the PEN/Revson Fellowship and the Paterson Poetry Prize. His poems have appeared in *The New York Times Book Review*, *Harper's*, *The Nation*, and *The Best American Poetry*. He is also the editor of *Poetry Like Bread: Poets of the Political Imagination from Curbstone Press* (Curbstone, 1994) and *El Coro: A Chorus of Latino and Latina Poetry* (University of Massachusetts Press, 1997). A recipient of fellowships from the National Endowment for the Arts and the Massachusetts Cultural Council, Espada is currently a Professor in the Department of English at the University of Massachusetts–Amherst.

About South End Press

South End Press is a nonprofit, collectively run book publisher with over 200 titles in print. Since our founding in 1977, we have tried to meet the needs of readers who are exploring, or are already committed to, the politics of radical social change. Our goal is to publish books that encourage critical thinking and constructive action on the key political, cultural, social, economic, and ecological issues shaping life in the United States and in the world. In this way, we hope to give expression to a wide diversity of democratic social movements and to provide an alternative to the products of corporate publishing.

Through the Institute for Social and Cultural Change, South End Press works with other political media projects— *Z Magazine*; Speakout, a speakers' bureau; Alternative Radio; and the Publishers Support Project—to expand access to information and critical analysis. If you would like a free catalog of South End Press books, please write to us at: South End Press, 7 Brookline Street, #1, Cambridge, MA 02139. Visit our website at http://www.lbbs.org.

Related Titles

*De Colores Means All of Us: Latina Views
for a Multi-Colored Century*
by Elizabeth Martínez

The Last Generation: Poetry and Prose
by Cherríe Moraga

*Colonial Dilemma: Critical Perspectives
on Contemporary Puerto Rico*
edited by Edwin Meléndez and Edgardo Meléndez

The Shock of Arrival: Reflections on Postcolonial Experience
by Meena Alexander